'This book provides several new perspectives on professionalism, which I look forward to thinking through in depth.'

Michael Eraut, Professor Emeritus, University of Sussex

'This is an exceptionally interesting collection of essays on a theme of central significance in contemporary education. The range of perspectives is broad, the questions addressed are complex and the analysis is incisive. It is further evidence of the emerging significance of the professional doctorate (the origin of these contributions was lectures to such a programme) and the Institute of Education is to be congratulated on making the results available to a wider audience.'

Professor William Richardson, University of Exeter

'These are testing times for the professions. They are widely regarded politically as roadblocks to modernisation and reform and governments have legislated accordingly. As a consequence of this, we have seen the steady incorporation of professionalism into managerialism as a mode of organising work in complex and social and economic systems. It is thus an appropriate time to give deep consideration to the future of the professions. This has been admirably fulfilled in this collection. The issues of professional knowledge, institutions, power, ethics, work-patterns and identities are explored afresh in this scholarly work.'

Eric Hoyle, Emeritus Professor of Education, University of Bristol

The Bedford Way Papers series

A full list of Bedford Way Papers, including earlier books in the series, may be found at www.ioe.ac.uk/publications

Exploring Professionalism

Edited by Bryan Cunningham

Foreword by Sir David Watson

Bedford Way Papers

First published in 2008 by the Institute of Education, University of London,
20 Bedford Way, London WC1H 0AL
www.ioe.ac.uk/publications

© Institute of Education, University of London 2008

British Library Cataloguing in Publication Data:
A catalogue record for this publication is available from the British Library

ISBN 978 0 85473 805 2

Page make up by Hobbs the Printers Ltd, Totton, Hampshire SO40 3WX
Printed by Elanders www.elanders.com

Contents

Foreword by Professor Sir David Watson

Universities have always had an intimate relationship with the 'professions', not only producing 'professionals' but also creating and subjecting to rigorous critique the content of professional knowledge. In the later Middle Ages the relevant cast of disciplinary characters included lawyers and theologians, as well as (often forgotten) rhetoricians and musicians. In the early modern period public servants of various kinds ('administrators') were added to the mix. In the great age of higher education foundations of the late nineteenth and early twentieth centuries, science and technology (broadly understood – to include, for example, architecture) had their day in the sun. In the late twentieth century the various professions of the service and creative economies joined in. In this phase many complex occupations previously characterised as 'craft' (for example art and design) achieved appropriate recognition of their role within the higher education enterprise. Law and medicine (latterly health more generally) have been there throughout, as have educators of various kinds since the nineteenth century. The early twenty-first century has followed the postmodernist spirit of the times by adding to the professional palette new domains such as capital markets, niche journalism, alternative therapies and call-centre management.

But what about the professionalism of higher education (HE) itself? Where are the standards, the peer recognition, the discipline, the attention to 'fitness to practise', the expectation of personal and professional updating within HE-based teaching and research? While contributing to the development of the range of professional occupations, through both initial formation (licence to practise) and continuous professional development (CPD), higher education itself has probably been (until recently in this long and rich story) relatively unselfconscious about its own processes and priorities.

However, our world is changing, and Bryan Cunningham and his fellow authors have caught a distinct wave. The essays collected here cover a rich mixture of internal perspectives – on how higher education serves professions of various kinds in their requirements for better-grounded knowledge, technique and judgement – and external pressures – such as those of the 'market', of a welcome 'ethical turn' in public life, and of the 'supercomplex' conditions of contemporary knowledge generation, testing and application. The development of professional doctorates – such as the Education Doctorate (EdD) for which much of this material was generated – is a demonstration of the legendary adaptability of higher education to changed contexts and new demands.

Within the HE tent the objective remains one with a strong historical pedigree: to assist professionals of all types to perform with confidence, with appropriate regard for the wider consequences of their actions, with a research-informed sense of reflexivity or self-knowledge, and with a sense of stewardship of the professional field to which they belong. Exploring Professionalism makes a significant contribution to each of these goals and deserves to be widely read across the contemporary professional scene.

Professor Sir David Watson is Professor of Higher Education at the Institute of Education, University of London. Between 1990 and 2005 he was Vice-Chancellor of the University of Brighton. He is joint author (with Hazel Bines) of *Developing Professional Education* (Open University Press, 1992) and editor (with Tim Katz and Tom Bourner) of *New Directions in Professional Higher Education* (Open University Press, 2000).

Preface

This book grew out of *Foundations of Professionalism* at the Institute of Education, University of London. This course effectively forms the introduction to a part-taught Doctorate in Education (EdD) programme. As with the professional doctorates (PDs) offered at other universities this is being followed by increasing numbers of senior professionals with backgrounds not only in mainstream education, or even the public sector, but in fields as diverse as medicine and dentistry, architecture, social work, consultancy and international development.

The proposal to create a single volume bringing together the diverse perspectives on professional life had been discussed at various points in the history of *Foundations of Professionalism*. There were probably two main reasons behind its finally coming to fruition. First, it was becoming evident that, with the spread across universities of PDs, there could well be a need for a volume that might serve as a reader, inducting new students into the range of perspectives from which professional life might be viewed, and into the tools and discourses employed in its analysis. No such volume appeared to have been called into being by the growth in interest in EdD-type programmes. Second, there arose the question of whether it could be seen as simply wasteful that so many high-quality lecture inputs as were being made to the 'Foundations' course might be at risk of being 'lost' (except, of course, to those who had actually heard them), especially as key contributors moved 'onwards and upwards' or retired from academic life.

The rationale for *Exploring Professionalism* is thus to preserve, and make accessible to a wider audience, a rounded selection of perspectives on professional life, as offered by some of the UK's most distinguished scholars in the field. It is hoped that the papers will be found of high value by individuals opting to work on a professional doctorate – where a focus on issues of professionalism in changing, challenging, times will be of prime importance. Additionally, however, it is our hope that the volume will find a broader readership from among those who, although they are not undertaking formal study (even, in fact, if they would not actually describe themselves as 'education professionals'), still possess a concern for, and a curiosity about, some of the issues currently exercising professionals who do earn their living in one or other of the extremely varied niches in education, in its most all-embracing sense.

Notes on the contributions

Exploring Professionalism has been written with the interests and concerns of a number of professional groups in mind. It seems fairly clear that a greater emphasis on inter-professional working carries with it the likelihood of specific 'professional issues' extending well beyond the bounds of schools, colleges or universities and into the professional realms of practitioners in fields as diverse as social work, educational psychology, health and law. We anticipate, therefore, that readers from a wide range of professions will readily locate within the respective contributions a number of issues, trends and scenarios that have resonance for them even if they themselves are employed outside education.

Further, even if we were only to contemplate what is occurring in mainstream education, the perspectives on professional life included here are all ones that we would claim hold strong relevance to all of the various sectors. While some authors may have special knowledge of, say, the secondary phase, others may draw quite substantially on illustrative material from higher education. Certain of us have particular interests – because of our professional backgrounds and present research activities – in what is happening in the further, adult and community education fields. However, it would be extremely unlikely that any particular issue or development described in this volume as having a significant impact on professionals in any one sector would be entirely unique to it. Indeed, a very notable feature of the discussions on *Foundations of Professionalism* over the years has been the numerous ways in which our course participants have identified 'crossover' issues; in some senses, the incidence of these has actually probably been increasing, with the advent of debates over such initiatives as a 14–19 curriculum, degree-awarding powers for further education colleges, and so on.

The volume opens with a paper contributed by two people, Deborah Andrews and Christine Edwards, who have themselves 'explored professionalism' through working towards, and successfully gaining, doctorates in education. Among the many valuable insights offered by the authors, I would highlight the way in which attention is drawn to encounters with the language of professional life – and of the study of professional life. One of the important transitions described in the paper is that of becoming empowered both to interpret and to interrogate this language – to probe beneath its exterior to ascertain its real meaning. Strong attention is also given to other 'consciousness-raising' dimensions of undertaking doctoral study. The hope is that, above all else, Andrews' and Edwards' paper motivates and inspires other readers to embark confidently on their own journey towards a professional doctorate.

Professional doctorates necessitate an early engagement with how the very notion of 'profession' originated and has subsequently evolved over time, and in different national and societal contexts. As David Crook makes clear, this does not merely entail a semantic debate; deploying a skilled historian's attention to detail, he valuably explores the ways in which over time our concept of 'the professions' has been subject to continuous change and contestation. Although conceding that 'it seems unlikely that application of historical perspectives will definitively settle arguments about whether particular occupations are professions', Crook helpfully elucidates a number of key themes that are evident from his examination of the rise over time of extremely diverse professional groups. Towards the end of an especially wide-ranging chapter, Crook also alludes to the possible 'postmodern' argument (not one that he himself would subscribe to) 'that we can all – dog-walkers and landscape gardeners no less than solicitors and archbishops – be professionals if we want to be'. More soberly, however, he reminds us that if measured by the yardstick of the published list of appropriate counter-signatories for UK passport applications, only some 49 professions appear to be 'secure'.

A wide variety of other 'lenses' is employed by our other contributors in their exploration of professionalism. There are those of Stephen Ball and Geoff Whitty, for example, which examine very closely indeed the sociological and political contexts in which education professionals operate. Whitty traces the important ways in which views of teacher professionalism have been shaped by major policy shifts in recent times. Certain policy initiatives have 'necessitated the growth of managerialism and the development of a distinct managerial tier within schools, one consequence of which is likely to be increased fragmentation of the profession'. Nevertheless, more positively he emphasises in particular the space that opens up – potentially at least – for a professionalism that is both collaborative and democratic; recent education reforms, he argues, far from precluding our being able to hope for a professional future may actually empower teachers and their learners.

Ball also takes as his canvas the notion of reform, and the ways in which, ultimately, the teacher is at the very heart of education reform. Many of the current manifestations of trends that enhance the accountability of teachers, and the marketisation of the education sector, are surely ones that will be recognisable to many from Ball's analysis of the evidence: being 'burdened with the responsibility to perform' seems to capture very well the tenor of life for many education professionals today. A number of forces – performativity and privatisation are those given special emphasis by Ball – are causing us to 'work on ourselves'; we are, 'at an individual level ... mostly left to struggle with the difficult dilemmas involving organisational self-interests being set over and against obligations to our students and "old" commitments like equity and fairness and scholarship'. These are surely generic changes; for a writer such as Ball, what seems clear is that the teachers cited by him are but a case in point – there is in fact very little that is unique to them in their professional 'enclave'.

Chapters such as those contributed by Sally Power and Louise Morley not only make reference to the major educational, indeed societal, shifts impacting on professional life in education, they also – to exploit further the metaphor of 'lenses' – zoom in on what is evident at the institutional and individual levels. Power in particular offers a convincing theorisation of, among other things, the manifest ways in which, for example, the kinds of organisational, managerial bullying that is, from the evidence, afflicting large numbers of individuals is a syndrome located 'in the wider orbit – not just the national but the international orbit'. Personal troubles, argues Power (drawing on C. Wright Mills' work), are more likely than not to be symptomatic of broader public issues. It is through the development of a 'professional imagination' that we can more fully understand such linkages, thereby better equipping ourselves to 'move beyond conceptions of ourselves and our work which either overemphasise or underplay individual capacity to effect change'.

Morley's chapter is important for several reasons, but here I will try to highlight two in particular. First, her examination of the micropolitics of professional life points up the huge inequalities and disadvantage that can result from the 'increasingly subtle and sophisticated ways in which dominance is achieved in organisations'. In arguing for a micropolitical literacy, Morley lucidly demonstrates how 'identifying one's own discomforts can provide valuable information about how wider systems of power operate'. Second, in drawing on some major research projects – including ones that she herself was involved in conducting – in locations as disparate as Scandinavia and sub-Saharan Africa, Morley provides strong evidence for 'the apparatus of micropolitics appear[ing] to have a transnational reach'.

Two contributions to the volume explore specific issues that have taken on a vastly enhanced importance for professionals in recent times. Ingrid Lunt's focus on ethical professionalism gives weight to the necessity for greater engagement by professionals with debates around probity, regulation and fitness to practise. In the 'risk society' that Lunt alludes to, the trust placed by society in professionals is in great jeopardy; 'the permanent features of uncertainty and unpredictability undermine what were previously considered professional certainties'. Furthermore, argues Lunt, 'the "blame and shame" culture can create a complex tension between professional loyalty and a search for the public good'. In such a context, professionals' demonstrable adherence to an ethical code carries great significance. But what form should an appropriately modern code take, and what status should it hold? There are, as well, broader questions and issues raised in Lunt's chapter; 'we need to embrace a more modern ethical professionalism', she argues, within a climate in which 'trust must be shown to be earned and deserved'.

Penny Jane Burke, meanwhile, takes as her focus what for many of us has been the single most significant policy steer for further and higher education in the UK since the 1990s – how are professionals in colleges and universities to assist the parallel government projects of widening participation (WP) and reducing social exclusion? Burke adopts an original stance in exploring the specific ways in which practitioners need to conceptualise the notion of widening participation, and to interrogate how, as informed, reflexive professionals, they act in ways that are both supportive and principled. For Burke, in the context of WP, professional identities come into play as significantly as do those of their students: 'the (multiple, fluid) identities of the new WP professional workforce matter and impact on decision-making processes, including the potential for serious questioning of what WP is'.

For Bryan Cunningham, reflexivity – being able to function as a learning professional – is of sufficient importance to warrant examination in its own right. Notwithstanding the twists and turns that we perceive we have travelled in arriving at our present notions of what constitutes a profession, and professionalism, most of us would probably accept the proposition that knowledge needs to feature somewhere. How professional knowledge is acquired, sustained and extended is Cunningham's major interest, and his chapter explores what for him is a crucial component of these processes. The 'critical incident' as a disturbance of professional equilibrium (even when to outward appearances the cause of the disequilibrium may be seemingly trivial events), often leading to a positive acceleration of professional learning, is the principal focus of this chapter.

Whatever dimension, or dimensions, of current professional life the individual contributors view as being of prime interest and importance, Ronald Barnett would argue that looming is a phenomenon he describes as supercomplexity. Professional life is now 'fraught with difficulty', and 'the ice cracks within' it, according to Barnett. Marketisation and regulation are but two features of this emergent state of affairs; a situation where 'clients' may increasingly feel empowered effectively to say to professionals 'I know as much as you do' is another. In such conditions 'the hard-pressed professional is faced with an identity crisis'. However, Barnett's chapter also presents us with some enticing conceptualisations of the professional's ability to confront all this by mastering the 'multiple discourses' of professional life, and by deploying his or her criticality and creativity.

Each of our contributing authors, then, while being concerned to acknowledge, and engage with, such major, overarching themes of modern professional life as change, challenge and an enhanced need for reflexivity and action, has focused on specific aspects of professionalism that they have played a significant role in researching over the course of their own professional careers. Overall, the collection of papers that has emerged is one that we believe will induct readers into certain of the key questions that they themselves may encounter as they begin their own exploration of 'professionalism'. For those actually undertaking formal studies through the EdD or other PD routes, there may be ideas here that will play a part in a process described by Andrews and Edwards, in the paper with which we open this volume – that of being 'pushed ... onto a different plane and provided ... with a continuing sense of challenge and achievement'.

Acknowledgements

I would wish to thank sincerely all of those colleagues at the Institute of Education and elsewhere who have found the time to contribute both to the *Foundations of Professionalism* programme at different times, and now to this present volume. I feel privileged to have worked over the past decade with such an incredibly distinguished group of scholars. From among them, I am particularly grateful to Professors Sally Power, Ingrid Lunt and Gary McCulloch, all of who played an important role, in their various ways, in giving me the confidence to embark on *Exploring Professionalism* in the first place.

In terms of the support I have had in actually getting the volume into print, Jim Collins of Bedford Way Papers should certainly be mentioned, and the editorial assistance of Claire Mills has been truly invaluable; Claire has, additionally, been of enormous importance for some years to the smooth running of *Foundations of Professionalism*.

Special thanks are also due to Caroline Daly for her most insightful comments on my own chapter; I have tried to incorporate certain important perspectives she felt the original lacked. Ronald Barnett's and Sarah Gardner's attention to stylistic detail has also improved my contributions to this book.

Bryan Cunningham,
February 2008

Contributors

Deborah Andrews

Deborah Andrews has worked in or around education since graduating in English from Oxford in the 1970s. She went from educational publishing into teaching and, since completing her doctorate at the Institute of Education, University of London, where her supervisor was Bryan Cunningham, has worked in widening participation in higher education, first at King's College London and now at Queen Mary University of London, where she is Peer Mentoring Coordinator. In her family, she is in the middle of three generations of teachers.

Stephen J. Ball

Stephen J. Ball is Karl Mannheim Professor of the Sociology of Education at the Institute of Education, University of London. His work is in 'policy sociology' and he has conducted a series of ESRC-funded studies which focus on issues of social class and policy. Recent books include *Education Plc* (Routledge, 2007) and *Education Policy and Social Class* (Routledge, 2006) and with Carol Vincent *Childcare Choice and Class Practices* (Routledge, 2005). He has an honorary doctorate from Turku University, is Visiting Professor at the University of San Andres and is a Fellow of the British Academy; for the last three years he has been an ESRC Fellow.

Ronald Barnett

Ronald Barnett is Pro-Director for Longer Term Strategy and Professor of Higher Education at the Institute of Education, University of

London. His work has been principally that of developing a social philosophy of higher education. His books include *The Idea of Higher Education* (Open University Press, 1990), *Realizing the University in an Age of Supercomplexity* (Open University Press, 2000) and *Beyond All Reason: Living with ideology in the university* (Open University Press, 2003). Just published is *A Will to Learn: Being a student in an age of uncertainty* (Open University Press, 2007).

Penny Jane Burke

Penny Jane Burke is Head of Department of Educational Foundations and Policy Studies at the Institute of Education, University of London. She is course tutor on the MA in higher and professional education, which offers a broad approach to understanding changes in higher education in relation to interdisciplinary theoretical frameworks, policy developments and professional practices. Dr Burke is the Chair of the Institute's Widening Participation Committee and leads the module 'Widening Participation: Policy and Practice'. She has published widely in the field, critically examining issues of access and participation from a sociological perspective. Her sole-authored book, *Accessing Education: Effectively widening participation* (Trentham, 2002), draws on ESRC-funded research, and has attracted significant press coverage and reviews in key educational journals. Her co-authored book (with S. Jackson) *Reconceptualising Lifelong Learning* is published by Routledge and was launched in May 2007.

David Crook

David Crook is Senior Lecturer in History of Education at the Institute of Education, University of London, a former Secretary of the UK History of Education Society and joint editor designate of *History of Education*. A former secondary school teacher, he has published widely, especially in the fields of selective and comprehensive secondary education and teacher training. He has recently edited (with Gary McCulloch) *History, Politics and Policy-Making: A Festschrift for Richard Aldrich* (Institute of Education, 2007) and is joint editor (also with Gary McCulloch) of *The Routledge International Encyclopedia of Education*.

Bryan Cunningham

Bryan Cunningham is Director of Quality Assurance and Enhancement in the Institute of Education, University of London's Faculty of Policy and Society. His other responsibilities include leading the EdD module 'Foundations of Professionalism', a programme he has been involved with for a decade, and making significant contributions in the area of lecturer training and development. He was formerly course leader for the master's in teaching and learning in higher and professional education. One of his areas of special interest is in mentoring; his text *Mentoring Teachers in Post-Compulsory Education* was the first available 'effective practice' guide for mentors in the UK further education colleges, and he has published a number of articles contextualised in this sector. In early 2008 he was a Visiting Scholar at the European University Institute, Florence.

Christine Edwards

Christine Edwards worked in London comprehensive schools and further education colleges for 16 years before joining the Open College Network, where she worked on developing access to higher education programmes. For the past five years Christine has taught on a number of teacher education programmes at the Institute of Education, University of London. She completed her doctorate through the EdD route, also at the Institute, and her research area is adult education and professional development.

Ingrid Lunt

Ingrid Lunt is Professor of Educational Psychology and Director of Graduate Studies at the University of Oxford, Department of Education. Prior to moving to Oxford, she was Dean of the Doctoral School at the Institute of Education, University of London. She has been involved in the EdD at the Institute of Education since its inception and has taught on 'Foundations of Professionalism' every year since the start of the programme. She has written extensively on professional aspects of psychology, in particular educational psychology, and is past President of the British Psychological Society, past President of the European Federation of Psychologists' Associations, and past Chair of the United Kingdom Inter-Professional Group. She is particularly interested in professional ethics and in higher professional learning. She co-directed an ESRC-funded research project on professional doctorates and their contribution to professional development and careers in 2002 (see Scott, D., Brown, A., Lunt, I. and Thorne, L. *Professional Doctorates: Integrating Professional and Academic Knowledge* Open University Press, 2004). She has recently completed an EU-funded project on European higher education and professional qualifications in psychology.

Louise Morley

Louise Morley is a Professor of Education and Director of the Centre for Higher Education and Equity Research (CHEER) at the University of Sussex. Her previous posts were at the Institute of Education, University of London, the University of Reading and the Inner London Education Authority. Louise has international interests in the field of sociology of higher education studies. She is currently directing a research project funded by the ESRC and the UK Department for International Development (DFID) on widening participation in higher education in Ghana and Tanzania (www.sussex.ac.uk/education/wideningparticipation). She has recently directed a DFID/Carnegie-funded research project on gender equity in Commonwealth higher education (www.ioe.ac.uk/efps/GenderEqComHE). In the UK, she has conducted policy research for the Higher Education Funding Council for England on establishing the needs of employers for information about the quality and standards of higher education provision (www.hefce.ac.uk/pubs/hefce/2006/06_45/). Some recent publications include *Gender Equity in Selected Commonwealth Universities,* Research Report No. 65 (DFID, 2006) and *Quality and Power in Higher Education* (Open University Press, 2003).

Sally Power

Before joining Cardiff University School of Social Sciences in 2004 as a Professorial Fellow, Sally Power was based at the Institute of Education, University of London, where she was head of the School of Educational Foundations and Policy Studies. During her time there, she was also Assistant Dean of Research and Publications and Chair of the Research Careers Advisory Committee. In addition to her own research interests in the area of education policy, she has extensive experience of working with professionals on a variety of master's and doctoral programmes. In addition to many papers and chapters on contemporary education policy, recent books include *Education and the Middle Class* (co-authored with T. Edwards, G. Whitty and V. Wigfall and published by Open University Press in 2003) and *Devolution and Choice in Education: The State, the school and the market* (co-authored with G. Whitty and D. Halpin and published by Open University Press in 1997).

Geoff Whitty

Geoff Whitty has been Director of the Institute of Education, University of London, since 2000. His main areas of teaching and research are the sociology of education, education policy and teacher education. He has led evaluations of major educational reforms in the UK, including the assisted places scheme, changes in initial teacher education and, most recently, provision for pupil voice in schools. He has also assisted schools and local authorities in building capacity for improvement. He is currently President of the College of Teachers, Immediate Past President of the British Educational Research Association, and a member of the General Teaching Council for England.

1 Consciousness in transition: the experience of doctoral study

Deborah Andrews and Christine Edwards

For two relatively recent recipients of Doctorates in Education (EdD), finding ourselves between pages filled by luminaries in our field feels a shade disconcerting but, we remember, we are all professionals – or are we? In this chapter we will explore how far studying for a professional doctorate has influenced our feelings on this question. We will consider the impact of taking a doctorate on our own professional lives. It is the story of the researchers rather than the story of the research: the pursuit of our separate stories becomes the story itself. This is not about what we actually researched but how we invented ourselves as researchers and how the professional insights gained from the EdD experience affected our personal and professional development. It explores self-identity, struggles and reflections. We will begin by considering our motivation for undertaking an EdD, touching briefly on our research areas, and then consider the effect it had on our perceptions of our professionalism, both during our studies and afterwards.

There are similarities in our stories. Both of us defined ourselves professionally before, during and after our doctoral studies as teachers, even though one of us was not a teacher when we began and one of us no longer is. We were both in our forties when we started the EdD, having reached a mid-career 'Reassessment Phase' (Hubermann, 1993: 8). Our professional lives, prompting our research, were set in the wider educational policy context of widening participation and qualifications reform. For one of us, undertaking the EdD was an attempt to channel frustration at the barriers, both actual and perceptual, that came between her A-level students and the academy. She 'knew', from wide experience and a wealth of anecdote, that these were harder for first-generation aspirants but had little theoretical underpinning to help bolster her arguments with the unconvinced. Anyway, she had found, in contrast to the enthusiastic reception for her well-meaning but superficially constructed views on education in her first career as an educational publisher, that people didn't listen to teachers. Perhaps, she thought, they listened to teachers with doctorates. For the other, the EdD was a way of putting the passion back into professional life that was being eroded by the soulless discourse of quality assurance cycles and appraisal and review systems. She had always believed (perhaps somewhat romantically) that as a teacher quality was self-imposed and felt boxed into a corner by those all around who seemed better able to cope, at least on the outside, with being constantly monitored and audited. She felt the EdD would help resolve an inner turmoil that had begun to create professional uncertainty and insecurity.

We both chose to take professional doctorates, rather than PhDs, mainly because of the stimulation of collaborative working we perceived we would encounter as part of a cohort. The pleasure we found in meeting each other, sharing ideas and complexities and often working on joint presentations during our studies was perhaps underpinned by recognising in each other a determination never to reach the phase of 'disenchantment' and 'disinvestment' in any career. We had also a restlessness that makes us disinclined to aspire to 'serenity' (Huberman, 1993) either. Epistemologically, we were two ticks in the same box, both taking an interpretive approach to our research to allow to be heard the voices of those whose views are not usually dominant in policy documents. As the course progressed, the writings of the same people struck a chord against our own thinking and research – Alison Wolf, John Eliot, Martin Hammersley, Stephen Ball and Frank Coffield. Out of these similarities, in professional life stage and academic interests, emerged both an energising sense of partnership and a friendship. This served as strength and inspiration in our EdD work.

Having reached mid-career, we both had a strong professional identity of being teachers and both had considerable experience of running departments. We found ourselves, however, constantly seeking out new challenges with a strong need to emerge with projects of a certain significance, what Hubermann refers to as the 'experimentation and diversification phase' of the teacher's life cycle (1993: 7). We have mentioned earlier that neither had been a teacher all her life, though both had worked always in education, with an early career in publishing for one and a pre-EdD shift from teaching to training and staff development for the other. It was during one of these periods of reassessment of our future life course and, perhaps, self-doubt that, for both of us, an EdD found its way onto the balance sheet of what was still possible. It was an attractively new development yet one that kept coherence with what we had done before.

The choice most certainly goes deeper than the normative and deterministic explanation offered by the life cycle analysis, fascinating though it is to apply this to one's career in retrospect. We suspect it has roots in the clash of ideologies brought about by the external forces of the government's policy of modernisation in public services. For those of us working in the post-compulsory sector, this involved a shift towards a managerialist approach with its reductionist values and audit culture (Shain and Gleeson, 1999: 456). A new way of thinking permeated the system in which we worked and became the unchallenged dominant discourse; those of us not fully convinced felt we were constantly playing off-side. Unhappy at the internalisation of reflexivity, we questioned where we were good enough in terms of performativity measures. Our common sense told us something was wrong. When making sense of our world is no longer a matter of common sense, Gramsci (1971) argues, philosophy provides 'intellectual order' and 'critical awareness', and this is certainly what we needed at the time.

Definitions of professionalism will be explored elsewhere in this book, suffice it to say here that given that a key definer of 'professional' is someone with advanced training in a particular area, a doctorate should make one a 'more professional' teacher. While time does not allow us to deal with worms released from cans, we relate more closely to the nature of the term as bestowing approval: 'worthy of or appropriate to a professional person; competent' (Oxford English Dictionary). From this perspective, the effect on our own view of ourselves as professionals was greatest *during* our studies. Giving ourselves permission to make time and space for professional development was in itself recognition that the issues concerning us all our working lives, on which we now had time to reflect, had worth and *gravitas*. The backed-up store that had accumulated from all the 'thinking on the hoof' that was a characteristic of our hectic professional lives could now be unscrambled, assessed and considered, a process approved by Hargreaves and Goodson (1996: 20–1) as one of the strands in what 'teacher professionalism should [also] mean ... a self-directed search and struggle for *continuous learning* related to one's own expertise and standards of practice, rather than compliance with the enervating obligations of *endless change* demanded by others'.

It was tempting at first to think of oneself as a deficit model (particularly 'not a statistician') but, gradually, we began to move forward with more confidence, relishing the broad nature of this educational research discipline we had entered and to configure and draw upon our primary disciplines and those of our student colleagues. We realised that being a geographer gave insight into problem solving and theoretical analysis and that having a degree in English did not just make you the one who found writing assignments less daunting but also gave ready access to metaphor as a research tool.

Becoming practitioner researchers in our own workplaces made the familiar new. One of us felt that although her advancing research skills made her more sceptical of, and more irritated by, the lack of rigour in what Coffield (2003) describes as 'the unscientific world of educational consultants, whose Powerpoint presentations are all colour and no content, and whose conclusions have no basis in research', she also found that many of her assumptions about the thoughts and motives around her in her workplace did not stand up to the scrutiny of her own research. This gave her habits of humility that have been carried forward, since completing her doctorate, into a new professional area. As Hargreaves and Goodson (1996: 13) observe, the teacher who 'just *knows*' is not necessarily *right*, for 'it depends on what knowledge is, in what contexts it has been acquired, the purposes to which it has been put, and the extent to which teachers review, renew and reflect on it.'

In an educational environment where 'excellence' is set as a goal and 'world class' standards are demanded as the norm, it can feel as if there is little space for taking risks. We are expected to set our targets and have the skills to achieve them. But in education we don't always know what the outcomes will be, they only emerge as part of the process, some good, some bad. Teachers need to feel on ground safe enough to take risks that may be creative and lead to genuine excellence, rather than settling for the false security that all ticks have been marked against a list of their competencies. The EdD has helped give us the confidence to continue taking risks.

In our experience many working in education seemed to have lost their sense of humour, some perhaps through complacency or even fear but others seemed to have deemed it inappropriate within a kind of *faux* professionalism. They were playing the system: perceiving that this is what is expected, engaging in a kind of cynical or strategic compliance (Ball, 2003: 222). Too often these *faux* professionals cover themselves in a cloak of jargon and if the EdD has helped us maintain the humour that enabled the small boy in the crowd to laugh at the nudity of the emperor, then it was perhaps worth it for this alone. Research and the reflection it stimulates provide a bulwark against the semantic swamping of jargon, and the discursive learning that takes place on the EdD entails a more or less constant manipulation and interrogation of language. We owe it to our students to become expert in this language but we owe it to them also to maintain our confidence in our professional instincts and to recognise the difference between jargon as a useful tool and as a sorcerer's apprentice, glutted on baseless power. Fielding is right to see dangers lurking:

> the very language we now use to talk about our work in education has changed, making it difficult to grasp aspects of our experience and our aspiration unless they fit readily into the cash nexus or the outcome measure ... we not only tend to see the world through a semantic lens which is distorting and dangerous. We are also likely to find ourselves behaving in surprising and unpleasant ways. If we really do come to think that we can 'deliver' the curriculum as we constantly say we can, then we are likely to find ourselves instructing more than we intend to and listening less than we should.
>
> (Fielding, 1999: 76)

The EdD led both of us away from teaching in the post-compulsory sector, although we remain closely linked to it in different ways. One of us has moved into the field of widening participation in a large London university and the other into teacher education, training teachers for the post-compulsory sector on a PGCE course. We do not regard ourselves as academics; having the vocational version of a PhD might prevent our acceptance into those ranks, even if we sought it. As elsewhere in the educational arena, there is movement but no closure towards the parity of esteem between the vocational and the academic. We believe, however, that the value of the EdD is in its difference, a positive choice rather than a less valued version of a PhD. We maintain, indeed, that the documented experience of insider research is likely to be the greatest contribution the doctorate In education will make to research as a whole. Local, professional knowledge makes the EdD researcher perceptive towards the micro, with the range and rigour of her wider doctoral studies enabling her to set this against the stretch of the macro, rising to the challenge summarised by Ball (1994: 15).

The challenge is to relate together analytically the *ad hocery* of the *macro* with the *ad hocery* of the *micro* without losing sight of the systematic bases and effects of *ad hoc* social actions: to look for the iterations embedded within chaos.

The EdD has given greater insight into the wider changes in society that have occurred since the end of the nineteenth century and an understanding of how they have affected education and, in turn, our own professional lives. We feel able to step back, to theorise, to engage with reflexivity rather than letting it leave us baffled and frustrated. We are able to draw on a knowledge base developed through the extensive reading undertaken during our studies and this continues to help make our professional lives more stimulating.

Perhaps the most valuable element of the EdD experience has been the way it forced us to engage with increasing levels of reflexivity during our studies. This was, at times, disruptive but has given us greater insight into ourselves as professionals and our ability to articulate what it means to be a professional in postmodernity. It has helped also to give us the courage to stand by the values in education that we feel are important and also to understand how we came by these values and what significance they have in the way we conduct our research and, indeed, our lives. Enhanced salaries have not been an outcome of our EdD experiences. The non-financial rewards, such as those we have been illustrating, have for us been greater. For some other EdD students reading this, the thoughts outlined in this chapter may resonate; others may have experienced it in different ways. In whatever way each individual engages with the professional doctorate, however, it will become part of that person's lifelong learning (Leonard and Coate, 2006). As avid lifelong learners, the EdD has pushed us onto a different plane and provided us with a continuing sense of challenge and achievement.

In reflecting on her doctoral studies, one of us said she hoped that the process of reflection would stay with her to continue to confer a sense of objectivity that made professional challenges less overwhelming. While she has found this to be the case, it has also occurred that in moving into a new field, widening participation, which is emergent in terms of professionalisation, her embedded sense of professionalism has been sufficiently robust to carry forward. Just as she learnt to have a sense of identity and purpose as an English graduate with sociological research, so she is learning to be a teacher within widening participation, pursuing outreach activities in a 'teacherly' fashion. Leaving teaching requires an adaptation to a sense of loss, to the feeling of freefall expressed by the New York English teacher interviewed by Goodson (2003: 70): 'There's a rhythm, there is a structure, there's a set of gestures, and there's a stance that's part of the job that is in my fibre.'

The sense that one has a profession, a 'competence', is not something that fades with moving on. Greater perhaps than the outward changes to our positions in the world of education have been the changes in our 'inner life' as educators brought about by the EdD. It has given us the personal and professional development to allow us to reclaim our identity as educational professionals.

References

Ball, S.J. (1994) *Education Reform*. Buckingham: Open University Press.

Ball, S.J. (2003) 'The teacher's soul and the terrors of performativity'. *Journal of Education Policy*, 18 (2): 215–28.

Coffield, F. (2003) 'Save Big L from the pop psychologists'. *Guardian* (Further Education Supplement), 21 November.

Fielding, M. (1999) 'Communities of learners'. In B. O'Hagan (ed.) *Modern Educational Myths*. London: Kogan Page.

Goodson, I.F. (2003) 'The personality of change'. In I.F. Goodson and A. Hargreaves (eds) *Professional Knowledge, Professional Lives*. Berkshire: Open University Press.

Gramsci, A. (1971) *Selections from the Prison Notebooks of Antonio Gramsci*. Edited and translated by Q. Hoare and G. Nowell Smith. London: Lawrence and Wishart.

Hargreaves, A. and Goodson, I.F. (1996) 'Teachers' professional lives: aspirations and actualities'. In A. Hargreaves and I.F. Goodson (eds) *Teachers' Professional Lives*. London: Falmer Press.

Hubermann, M. (1993) *The Lives of Teachers*. Translated by J. Neufeld. London: Cassell.

Leonard, D. and Coate, K. (2006) 'PhD as lifelong learning'. Paper given at BERA, University of Warwick, September.

Shain, F. and Gleeson, D. (1999) 'Under new management: changing conceptions of teacher professionalism and policy in the further education sector'. *Journal of Education Policy*, 14 (4): 445–62.

2 Some historical perspectives on professionalism
David Crook

Introduction

In September 1973 the Brussels Sheraton Hotel was the location for the third international conference on corporate planning. Among the delegates, uncertainty was in the air. Was corporate planning the efficient secret of leading-edge global businesses? Would the demand for their services from the world's leading companies be sustained, or was corporate planning in peril of being de-mystified and of reverting to a line management task? The keynote speaker was Dr Warren Bennis, who, from his base at the Massachusetts Institute of Technology in the 1960s, had conducted pioneering research into corporate leadership and the management of change. On the matter of whether corporate planning is a profession, Bennis was clear: 'The less said about it the better. No secure profession has sessions on whether it is a profession' (reported in *The Times*, 24 September 1973: 20).

It seems unlikely that application of historical perspectives will definitively settle arguments about whether particular occupations are professions. Studying the past can, however, shed light upon the contested nature of such terms as profession, professional and professionalism, and about continuities and change over time. In that spirit, the remainder of this chapter is divided into four parts. The next section examines the rise of the professional over time, focusing

10

especially on the so-called classical or learned professions. This is followed by an examination of how the concepts of professionalism and professionalisation have been approached by sociologists, historians and professionals themselves. While noting the formation of new professional groups, it is argued that the classical professions maintained their leading market position. There follows a discussion of how professionalisation has been influenced by interactions between amateurs and professionals. Current concerns about the 'cult of the amateur' are contrasted with past anxieties about the dangers of professionalism. The concluding section notes the democratisation of professionalism over time, but also tentatively asks whether this has been at the expense of intellectual leadership.

The rise of the professional

The concept of the specialist professional is identifiable from the Middle Ages, with churchmen, educated in cathedral schools, being the most prominent group. As European monarchs and overlords consolidated their positions, physicians and surgeons attended to their personal health, while jurists and bureaucrats facilitated the development of the modern state. By the twelfth and thirteenth centuries, 'governance [in Europe] was becoming the province of the bureaucrat and the professional' (Given, 1997: 91). As practices of diplomacy developed, the position of ambassador emerged as a further profession, and, underpinning all these arrangements, retained 'professional' armies maintained the social order. There were other specialists appointed to the courts of medieval Europe, too: cooks, jongleurs, minstrels and woodsmen, for example. For the masses, a barber, supplementing his normal work of trimming hair and shaving beards, often performed surgical procedures and teeth extractions. Other 'semi-professionals' included practitioners of folk medicine and midwives (Singman, 1999: 56).

A select group of Italian and French universities played the leading role in shaping the so-called classical professions of medicine, law and theology. The University of Salerno was founded in the ninth century by four masters (according to legend) – Helinus the Jew, Pontus the Greek, Adela the Arab, and Salernus the Roman – whose personal backgrounds provided the preconditions for its success in attracting students from a wide range of countries and cultures (Buck, 1917: 244). Similarly, the prominence of the University of Montpellier in the field of medicine from the thirteenth century was attributed to the fusion of Latin, Greek, Arab and Hebrew medical traditions. Meanwhile, the University of Bologna, founded in 1088, had become the leading centre for the education and training of lawyers, and the University of Paris, founded in the twelfth century, specialised in theological study. High-level studies in the medieval English universities of Oxford and Cambridge privileged these areas too, though with canon law and civil law based in separate faculties (Aldrich, 1996: 27). This medieval association in the West between the learned professions, the church and the university emphasised the distinction between professional elites and traders and artisans. The latter groups acquired their practical skills through apprenticeships, while a liberal university education, with teaching and study in Latin, was for gentlemen professionals (Larson, 1977: 4).

In Britain, it was centuries before this elite categorisation of professionals was challenged, though subdivisions emerged. The English essayist, Joseph Addison, son of the Dean of Lichfield, was sceptical about whether the specialist sub-branches of the professions were necessary, wondering how many country curates could have made a greater contribution and gained more personal fulfilment if they had been guided towards a career in trade or commerce. In 1711 he argued in *The Spectator* that 'the three great professions of divinity, law and physic' were 'over-burdened with practitioners', citing the inflation of honours within the church, mocking lawyers who never practised at the bar and those who 'frequent the playhouse more than Westminster-hall, and are seen in all public assemblies, except in a court of justice'. Within the field of medicine, Addison argued, there were

> innumerable retainers to physic, who, for want of other patients, amuse themselves with the stifling of cats in an air-pump, cutting up dogs alive, or impaling insects upon the point of a needle for microscopical observations; besides those that are employed in the gathering of weeds, and the chace of butterflies: not to mention the cockleshell-merchants and spider-catchers.
>
> (Addison, 1711: 65–8)

By the mid-nineteenth century more significant changes were under way to broaden the range of professional groups across Western Europe and North America. Commenting on British developments in this period, Noel Annan wrote:

> Not only were the old professions expanding to include attorneys and apothecaries, but the establishment in 1828 of the Institution of Civil Engineers to further 'the art of directing the Great Sources of Power in Nature for the use and convenience of mankind' marked the rise of a new kind of professional man. Members of these intellectual families became the new professional civil servants at a time when government had become too complicated and technical to be handled by the ruling class and their dependents. They became school inspectors or took posts in the museums or were appointed secretaries of philanthropic societies; or they edited or wrote for the periodicals or entered publishing houses; or, as journalists ceased to be hacks scribbling in Grub Street, they joined the staff of *The Times*. Thus they gradually spread over the length and breadth of English intellectual life, criticising the assumptions of the ruling class above them and forming the opinions of the upper middle class to which they belonged.
>
> (Annan, 1999: 10–11).

Annan's own particular interest was the emergence of the secular university academic, effectively a new profession in Britain, as suggested by the title of Engel's 1983 book *From Clergyman to Don*.

The professionalisation of higher education was a feature of many other countries in this period, too. In France, academic posts rose from about 570 in 1865 to 2,200 in 1919, and in Germany from 1,504 to 3,838 during the period 1873 to 1910. In most countries, professors and other academics were civil servants, with career opportunities for the finest scholars to progress to positions in the most prestigious universities, such as Paris or Vienna. While this was not the case for Oxford and Cambridge, the founding of new civic universities in the late nineteenth century enabled Oxbridge academics to take up new posts elsewhere, kick-starting the job market in this profession (Anderson, 2004: 137). A range of more specialised university institutions also emerged, driven by the forces of meritocracy, urbanisation, industrialisation, imperialism, modernisation and scientific rationality. The first modern business school, the École Supérieure de Commerce de Paris, was founded in 1819, providing a model for later American institutions, including the Harvard Business School and the University of Chicago Graduate School of Business. From 1910 and 1920, respectively, these institutions pioneered master of business administration and doctoral business programmes. The École Libre des Sciences Politiques, again in Paris, and the London School of Economics, meanwhile, were founded in 1872 and 1895 to define and serve elite professionals in the arenas of politics, public administration and commerce. The Massachusetts Institute of Technology had originally been opened in 1861, and, to celebrate its move to a new campus in 1916, 'floats sponsored by the major corporations of early 20th-century America chugged down the streets of Nantasket Beach in honor of a university designed in large part to serve the technical needs of American industry' (Brint, 1994: 8).

It was common for occupational groups seeking recognition as professions to mobilise under the umbrella of an association, institute or other body. The battle for acceptance was, in part, a matter of public relations, a point that was well understood by the American journalists who founded *Editor & Publisher* in 1901. This was not to be a trade magazine, but rather a *professional* magazine. From the outset, *Editor & Publisher* 'supported such emerging professionalizing agents as journalism schools, professional organizations, and ethics codes' (Cronin, 1993: 235). Seeking the public's trust, it promoted political independence, accuracy, fair play and even, as a 1912 editorial sought, the licensing of journalists:

> No one is allowed to practice medicine unless he possesses a diploma certifying that he has completed the course of study prescribed by a reputable medical college; no one can practice law unless he has been admitted to the bar after a searching examination; but anybody can engage in the practice of journalism without preparation and therefore without experience of any kind.
>
> (quoted in Cronin, 1993: 235)

On the other side of the world, journalists were, together with doctors, lawyers, accountants, engineers and professors, officially identified as elite professionals by the Chinese Guomindang in 1929, and the Shanghai Journalists Association was subsequently to play a key part in transforming the image of this group from that of 'literary men' to professionals. Until 1929 there had, in fact, been no Chinese word to distinguish 'profession' from 'occupation' (Xu, 2001: 2, 179).

Professionalism and professionalisation

In *The Acquisitive Society* (1920), the British socialist intellectual, R.H. Tawney, differentiated between industry and a profession. Industry, he argued, was principally concerned with providing returns to shareholders, but the measure of professionals' success 'is the service which they perform, not the gains which they amass':

> They may, as in the case of a successful doctor, grow rich; but the meaning of their profession, both for themselves and for the public, is not that they make money but that they make health, or safety, or

knowledge, or good government or good law. They depend on it for their income, but they do not consider that any conduct which increases their income is on that account good. . . .

So, if they are doctors, they recognize that there are certain kinds of conduct which cannot be practised, however large the fee offered for them, because they are unprofessional; if scholars and teachers, that it is wrong to make money by deliberately deceiving the public . . .; if judges or public servants, that they must not increase their incomes by selling justice for money; if soldiers, that the service comes first, and their private inclinations, even the reasonable preference of life to death, second. Every country has its traitors, every army its deserters, and every profession its blacklegs. To idealize the professional spirit would be very absurd; it has its sordid side, and, if it is to be fostered in industry, safeguards will be needed to check its excesses. But there is all the difference between maintaining a standard which is occasionally abandoned, and affirming as the central truth of existence that there is no standard to maintain.

(Tawney, 1920: 94–5)

From the 1930s, the notion of a profession became subjected to more systematic analyses. In a seminal text focusing on the British experience, Carr-Saunders and Wilson stopped short of providing a definition, but advised that the distinguishing mark of a professional is the possession of 'an intellectual technique acquired by special training', and that 'a profession can only be said to exist when there are bonds between the practitioners, and these bonds can take but one shape – that of the formal association (Carr-Saunders and Wilson, 1933: 200, 298). Other works pointed to a profession having at least some of the following traits: an extended and systematic preparation with an intellectual component taught in an institutional setting that upholds quality and competence; an expectation of its members to observe norms or codes of conduct; an emphasis upon service to others ahead of personal reward; an expectation that its members will demonstrate a high level of personal integrity. Later, academic opinion divided over the question of whether this type of 'attribute

16

model', which defines professions in terms of what professionals do, and how they conduct themselves, is useful. As an alternative, some favoured a 'process model' that is more sensitive to the power exercised by professionals to legitimate their primacy (e.g. Parsons, 1954; Greenwood, 1988: 12–14).

Professionalisation was variously viewed as a development that destroyed the integrity of Eastern European communism (Djilas, 1955), a by-product of meritocratic educational sorting that produces a new ruling class (Young, 1958) and, according to Larson's (1977) analysis of the United States and England, a capitalist instrument to take advantage of the university certification and legitimisation for the purpose of exercising bourgeois social control. Belatedly, perhaps, historians have joined these debates. For example, taking a more charitable approach than Larson, Haber (1991) argued that the professional power accumulated in the late nineteenth century by American lawyers, doctors and ministers of religion, as well as the newer groups of engineers and college professors, was exercised in a restrained, responsible and honourable manner, confirming these men to be the inheritors of the English gentry values. In relation to Britain and Germany, the past 20 years have witnessed the publication of impressive studies of British and German professionalisation by Perkin (1989), Cocks and Jarausch (1990), McClelland (1991) and Corfield (1995). This has not always been comfortable reading: in a brilliant and detailed analysis of the behaviour and practices of German lawyers, teachers and engineers in the first half of the twentieth century, Konrad Jarausch (1990) demonstrated how the most prominent associations to which these groups were affiliated publicly acclaimed Hitler's New Order. The explanation that professionals were simply caught unawares does not suffice, he maintains.

Two important points should be made at this juncture. The first is that the notion of trades stampeding to become recognised as professions in the late nineteenth and early twentieth centuries can be overplayed. An account of a 1936 conference of British drapers reported their pride in belonging to a trade, with its attendant emphasis upon customer care and satisfaction, rather than to a profession, though it was also noted that the area of retailing might, in time, be subject to professionalisation (*The Times*, 19 August 1936: 12). The second is that, beyond the classical fields of medicine, the law and the church, professionalisation of groups as diverse as engineers and scientists, nurses, teachers, corporate planners and personnel managers as a result of the mechanical, social and business 'revolutions' of the past 150 years has often been subject to comparative status differentiation. Using a contemporary scenario, those trained as doctors, nurses and paramedics are each likely to view themselves as dedicated professionals – indeed, each may have experienced a university education – but few would dispute that doctors are *primus inter pares*.

Industrial sociology may point here to the need for a more sophisticated typology, acknowledging proto-professionals and paraprofessionals, as well as more established professional groups. The modern social worker, a role which has developed out of a Western voluntary tradition, often in the past undertaken by feminist activists seeking to provide relief, education, training and hope for the least-advantaged members of society, presents an interesting case. In the United States of America Abraham Flexner posed the question 'Is social work a profession?' (1915) some 45 years before a 1960 British House of Lords debate about the welfare state. In this debate, Lord Pakenham – shortly to become the Earl of Longford – conceded that a qualification in social work could never be on the same footing as one in law, theology or accountancy, though he did see an analogy between training as a social worker and training as a teacher (*The Times*, 18 February 1960: 17). In similar vein, Burton R. Clark confirmed in 1962 that such professions as agriculture, business administration, dentistry, education, engineering, forestry, librarianship, nursing, optometry, pharmacy, public health and social welfare were 'struggling up the slope' and still trailing behind law and medicine (Clark, 1962: 82–3). In the instance of business management, even now apparently still struggling up the slope, one recent interpretation maintains that its failure to obtain undisputed recognition as a profession 'should not be seen as an outcome of it being "the wrong kind of knowledge"', but rather consequence of the classical professions achieving monopolistic closure (Grey, 2004: 51).

Amateurism and professionalism

In his bestselling *The Cult of the Amateur* (2007), Andrew Keen points to various examples of how 'Web 2.0' technologies have made it possible for ordinary people – 'amateurs' – to create blogs, share homemade videos, post Web pages, amend Wikipedia pages and so forth. In the United Kingdom, the growth of online banking and insurance and the showcasing of homes for sale has led to the partial withdrawal of some financial institutions and estate agents from the high street. More tellingly, perhaps, major record labels, including EMI, have issued profits warnings and announced staff redundancies in consequence of young people preferring to download music – often illegally – from the Web, rather than purchase CDs. Video and DVD rental stores are also said to be feeling the pinch as television and movie downloads have burgeoned. If amateurs are the winners, now ruling the Internet and undermining the culture and the economy, it follows that professionals – if it is accepted that those who work in financial services, retail stores, marketing executives and so on *are* professionals – are the losers.

Historically, this kind of discourse, emphasising the creeping threat of amateurs undermining professionals and professionalism is fascinating. It presents a 180-degree contrast to the situation of a century ago, and even more recently, when the concept of professionalism was viewed less benignly. Elizabeth Keeney has shown how, in the United States, amateur botanists, especially in Boston and New York, were upset when academics began to found societies that restricted membership to professionals, ending a period of peaceful and productive co-existence (Keeney, 1992: 37). Similarly, in 1891, Richard Norman Shaw, architect of the original Scotland Yard and of several theatres in London's West End, arguably the finest British-born architect of all time, protested that the Royal Institute of British Architects was influenced too much by men of business. These sinister forces, he maintained, were seeking 'to transform architecture from an art into a close profession by the introduction of examinations and diplomas' (letter, *The Times*, 11 November 1891: 4).

Nowhere was the threat of professionalism felt more keenly than in the area of sport. During its first 11 years, from 1872, the English Football Association Challenge Cup was won by Wanderers (five times), Old Etonians (twice), Clapham Rovers, Old Carthusians, Oxford University and the Royal Engineers. These were amateur teams of unpaid ex-public-school players, though many of these men were professionals in another walk of life. None of these teams reached the Cup Final again. Professional teams – initially Aston Villa, Blackburn Rovers, Preston North End and West Bromwich Albion – triumphed from 1883 and new controversies came to the fore about whether the introduction of player transfer fees, gate money, football pools and other forms of betting were destroying the game. Resisting the drift towards professionalisation, two proudly amateur clubs, Corinth and Casuals, were founded by alumni of the major round-ball-playing schools, later combining as Corinthian-Casuals. The Corinthians initially refused to enter competitions or to take penalties, embodying the public school ethos that 'the whole code of life is to play the game, that cheating is against the code, but that professionalism puts a man outside the code altogether' (*The Times*, 31 December 1929: 10; Taylor, 2006).

Controversy reigned in other sports, too. Jim Thorpe, the Native American winner of the decathlon and pentathlon gold medals at the 1912 Stockholm Olympics, was subsequently stripped of the medals when it emerged that, three years earlier, he had played minor league baseball in South Carolina, for which he had received small payments (Bruchac, 2006). As in association football, the engagement of 'hired men' divided English county cricket and, from the late 1870s, there were annual objections to the participation, and domination, of American 'amateur professional' rowers in the Henley Regatta (e.g. *New York Times*, 22 June 1879: 2). In 1901 Edmond Warre, Headmaster of Eton College, demanded the preservation of amateur oarsmanship from 'the deadly inroad of professionalism' (letter, *The Times*, 9 July 1901: 12).

The absence of professionalism in the British army officer class, it was widely maintained, was responsible for military catastrophes during the Boer War (*The Times*, 26 August 1903: 4). Similarly, in business, public-school boys were advised that they would have to abandon the amateurism that characterised those institutions if they were to succeed (*The Times*, 31 December 1929: 10). In the field of music, professionalism was viewed more positively by amateurs as the means of raising the standard of local choral and orchestral performance. Professionals were also encouraged to see benefits in working with, and developing, the amateurs who formed the nucleus of concert audiences (Shera, 1939; Kaplan, 1954). Indeed, this is an instance where professionals – composers, in particular – were beholden to amateurs to popularise their outputs. A witty poem, attributed to Mendelssohn, captured the composers' dilemma thus:

> If composers earnest are,
> Then we go to sleep;
> If they take a lively style,
> Then we vote them cheap;
> If the composition's long,
> Then its length we're fearing;

If the writer makes it short,
'Tisn't worth the hearing.
If the work is plain and clear,
Play it to some child;
If its style should deeper be,
Ah, the fellow's wild;
Let a man do as he will,
Still the critics fight;
Therefore let him please himself,
If he would do right.

(quoted in Kaplan, 1954: 26–7)

New professionals in certain other areas moved decisively during the nineteenth and twentieth centuries against the amateurs, hobbyists and dilettanti, though Stebbins (1992) and – using archaeology as a case study – Taylor (1995) have argued that spaces remained for amateurs to pursue 'serious leisure' in partnership with professionals. A major study of American medical practice has shown how this field became more scientific, professional and ethical (Warner, 1986), a process that advanced orthodox medical professionals at the expense of practitioners – dismissed as charlatans and 'quacks' – of alternative therapies, including homeopathy, osteopathy and acupuncture. According to Fournier (2002), professional market closure continues to impede the efforts of aromatherapists to gain legitimacy.

Unevenness and national variations accompanied the drive towards professionalisation in school teaching. In parts of Europe, teachers acquired civil servant status and entitlements to such professional benefits as pensions, but progress was impeded by the view – found in many countries – that 'good teachers are born and not made'. Where formal teacher training was endorsed, it was often maintained (and still is by some) that training 'on the job', following an apprenticeship model, is more suitable than programmes dependent upon university certification (see Herbst 1989; Robinson 2004). When, during the Second World War, it was decided that England and Wales should introduce an emergency training programme for teachers from the armed forces, lasting for one year rather than the normal two, Sir Ernest Graham-Little, Member of Parliament for the University of London, reasonably took the view that this represented a dilution that would never be asked of, or be acceptable to, the classical professions (letter, *Education*, 15 March 1946: 470). In more recent times, teachers have felt more assured, though rarely complacent, about their professional credentials. Donald Schön's (1983) concept of the 'reflective practitioner' had a special appeal to teachers and teacher educators, while such works as Hoyle and John (1995) and Whitty (2002) have conceptualised and theorised the professional nature of teachers' work, while also identifying overlapping, and sometimes competing, discourses about the nature of professionalism and 'professionality'.

Conclusion

Disappointingly, perhaps, the application of historical perspectives confirms professionalism to be an artificial construct, with ever-changing and always-contested definitions and traits. In times of late or postmodernity, some may wish to argue that we can all – dog-walkers and landscape gardeners no less than solicitors and archbishops – be professionals if we want to be professionals, and if we conduct ourselves in a manner that seems to be professional.

The period since about 1870 might be regarded as the long century of the professional. Since that time, the description has come to be applied not just to doctors, lawyers and clerics, but also to those who make their living as academics, accountants, investment bankers and librarians, among others. Recent additions might potentially include comedians, data analysts, directors of communication, personal trainers and Web designers. Professionals may also be found working in various capacities for charitable and non-governmental organisations. It remains the case, however, as Warren Bennis suggested 35 years ago, that only some professions – 49, at present for the purposes of a United Kingdom passport application countersignature – are 'secure', endowed with the requisite amount of social capital.

Recent efforts to define the modern professional have tended only to reinforce the plurality of understandings and interest groups. Brint's (1994) thesis, which argues that there has been a significant shift from social trust professionalism towards expert professionalism, is compelling, but does not fully capture the tensions between the ideal image of the modern professional (e.g. client-focused, independent, respectable, well rewarded, influential) and what is sometimes the reality (e.g. overwhelmed by paperwork, in peril of litigation, overworked, stressed). Status anxiety, to use Alain de Botton's (2004) term, seems now to have caught up with the group that once seemed exempt from it. Moreover, some recent writers have argued that the democratisation of the professions has diminished the intellectual leadership that professionals once provided (e.g. Said, 1994; Furedi, 2004). For the historian, this is certainly an area worth pursuing.

References

Addison, J. (1711) 'No. 21. Saturday, March 24'. *The Spectator*. In G.W. Greene (ed.) (1854), *The Works of Joseph Addison*, vol. V. New York: Putnam and Company.

Aldrich, R. (1996) *Education for the Nation*. London: Cassell.

Anderson, R.D. (2004) *European Universities from the Enlightenment to 1914*. Oxford: Oxford University Press.

Annan, N. (1999) *The Dons: Mentors, Eccentrics and Geniuses*. London: HarperCollins.

Brint, S. (1994) *In an Age of Experts: The Changing Role of Professionals in Politics and Public Life*. Princeton, NJ: Princeton University Press.

Bruchac, J. (2006) *Jim Thorpe, Original All-American*. New York: Dial.

Buck, A.H. (1917) *The Growth of Medicine from the Earliest Times to About 1800*. New Haven, CT: Yale University Press.

Carr-Saunders, A.M. and Wilson, P.A. (1933) *The Professions*. Oxford: Clarendon.

Clark, B.R. (1962) *Educating the Expert Society*. San Francisco, CA: Chandler.

Cocks, G. and Jarausch, K.H. (eds) (1990), *German Professions, 1800–1950*. Oxford: Oxford University Press.

Corfield, P.J. (1995) *Power and the Professions in Britain, 1700-1850*. London: Routledge.

Cronin, M.M. (1993) 'Trade press roles in promoting journalistic professionalism, 1884–1917'. *Journal of Mass Media Ethics*, 8(4): 227–38.

de Botton, A. (2004) *Status Anxiety*. London: Hamish Hamilton.

Djilas, M. (1955) *The New Class: An Analysis of the Communist System*. New York: Praeger.

Engel, A.J. (1983) *From Clergyman to Don: The Rise of an Academic Profession in Nineteenth-Century Oxford*. Oxford: Oxford University Press.

Flexner, A. (1915) 'Is social work a profession?'. *School and Society*, 1(26): 901–11.

Fournier, V. (2002) 'Amateurism, quackery and professional conduct: the constitution of "proper" aromatherapy practice'. In M. Dent and S. Whitehead (eds), *Managing Professional Identities: Knowledge, Performativity and the 'New' Professional*. London: Routledge.

Furedi, F. (2004) *Where Have All the Intellectuals Gone? Confronting 21st Century Philistinism*. London: Continuum

Given, J.B. (1997) *Inquisition and Medieval Society: Power, Discipline, and Resistance in Languedoc*. Ithaca, NY: Cornell University Press.

Greenwood, E. (1988) 'Attributes of a profession: revisited'. In S.K. Lal, U.J. Nahar, A. Chandani, and K. Khanna (eds), *Readings in the Sociology of the Professions*. Delhi: Gain.

Grey, C. (2004), 'Management as a technical practice: professionalisation or responsibilisation?'. In P. Jeffcutt (ed.), *The Foundations of Management Knowledge*. London: Routledge.

Haber, S. (1991) *The Quest for Authority and Honor in the American Professions, 1750–1900*. Chicago, IL: University of Chicago Press.

Herbst, J. (1989) *And Sadly Teach: Teacher Education and Professionalization in American Culture*. Madison, WI: University of Wisconsin Press.

Hoyle, E. and John, P. (1995) *Professional Knowledge and Professional Practice*. London: Cassell.

Jarausch, K.H. (1990) *The Unfree Professions: German Lawyers, Teachers and Engineers, 1800–1950*. Oxford: Oxford University Press.

Kaplan, M. (1954) 'The social role of the amateur'. *Music Educators Journal*, 40(4): 26–8.

Keen, A. (2007) *The Cult of the Amateur. How Today's Internet is Killing our Culture and Assaulting our Economy*. London: Nicholas Brealey.

Keeney, E.B. (1992) *The Botanizers: Amateur Scientists in Nineteenth-Century America*. Chapel Hill, NC: University of North Carolina Press.

Larson, M. (1977) *The Rise of Professionalism: A Sociological Analysis*. London: University of California Press.

McClelland, C.E. (1991) *The German Experience of Professionalization: Modern Learned Professions from the Early Nineteenth Century to the Hitler Era*. Cambridge: Cambridge University Press.

Parsons, T. (1954) 'The professions and social structure'. In *Essays in Sociological Theory*. New York: Free Press.

Perkin, H. (1989) *The Rise of Professional Society: England since 1880*. London: Routledge.

Robinson, W. (2004) *Power to Teach: Learning Through Practice*. Abingdon: Routledge.

Said, E. (1994) *Representations of the Intellectual*. London: Vintage.

Schön, D. (1983) *The Reflective Practitioner: How Professionals Think in Action*. London: Temple Smith.

Shera, F.H. (1939) *The Amateur in Music*. Oxford: Oxford University Press.

Singman, J.L. (1999) *Daily Life in Medieval Europe*. Westport, CT: Greenwood Press.

Stebbins, R. (1992) *Amateurs, Professionals, and Serious Leisure*. Montreal: McGill-Queen's University Press.

Tawney, R.H. (1920) *The Acquisitive Society*. New York: Harcourt, Brace and Howe.

Taylor, B. (1995) 'Amateurs, professionals and the knowledge of archaeology'. *British Journal of Sociology*, 46(3): 499–508.

Taylor, D.J. (2006) *On the Corinthian Spirit: The Decline of Amateurism in Sport*. London: Yellow Jersey Press.

Warner, J.H. (1986) *The Therapeutic Perspective: Medical Practice, Knowledge, and Identity in America, 1820–1885*. Cambridge, MA: Harvard University Press.

Whitty, G. (2002) 'Re-forming teacher professionalism for new times'. In *Making Sense of Education Policy*. London: Paul Chapman.

Xu, X. (2001) *Chinese Professionals and the Republican State: The rise of professional associations in Shanghai, 1912–1937*. Cambridge: Cambridge University Press.

Young, M. (1958) *The Rise of the Meritocracy, 1870–2033*. London: Thames and Hudson.

3 Changing modes of teacher professionalism: traditional, managerial, collaborative and democratic
Geoff Whitty

Introduction

Definitions of professionalism vary across time and place. This chapter focuses particularly on recent developments in teacher professionalism in England. Nevertheless, there are some increasing similarities between the education reforms being introduced in different parts of the world and we can learn from each others' approaches to, and understandings of, teacher professionalism. The chapter also concentrates on developments in the professionalism of school teachers, but much of the analysis may also be applicable to that of other education professionals.

An important issue for the professionalism of teachers is the nature of, and the limits to, teacher autonomy. Helsby and McCulloch (1996) pointed to the centrality of the classroom context in teachers' traditional claims to autonomy, arguing that:

> issues of curriculum control refer to teachers' rights and obligations to determine their own tasks in the classroom – that is, to the way in which teachers develop, negotiate, use and control their own knowledge – and are therefore central to teacher professionalism.
>
> (Helsby and McCulloch, 1996: 56)

Many years earlier, Lawton, a former director of the Institute of Education, similarly took the view that, in the classroom, the individual teacher's professional expertise and judgement should generally prevail (Lawton, 1980). However, the further one got away from the individual encounter in the classroom, he argued, the more other stakeholders needed to be involved in decision making. Thus, Lawton recognised that the claim of the profession to determine what counts as knowledge in the curriculum should be set alongside the rights of other stakeholders, including the elected government of the day.

More recent thinking has placed even greater emphasis on the role of other stakeholders, even within the classroom. It suggests, for example, that the active role of other adults such as parents and teaching assistants – and students themselves – is equally important in the development of appropriate learning environments (see, for example, Fielding, 1999). In England, this has become a key theme of education policy under New Labour – albeit as a reflection of the neo-liberal concern to restrict the voice of the teacher, rather than as an outright championing of other stakeholders as is the case in the literature on education and social justice.

This has certainly not led to a diminishing role for central government. Indeed, recent trends in decision making beyond the classroom have often restricted the extent to which teachers – and the other stakeholders just mentioned – have discretion. Furlong (2005) notes how in England the New Labour Government has established an alternative and increasingly dominant form of 'managerial professionalism', one which 'accepts that decisions about what to teach, how to teach and how to assess students are made at school and national level rather than by individual teachers themselves' (120). As Dainton (2005) concurs, New Labour's prescription, based in a 'quest for one-size-fits-all "what works" solutions' has played 'a powerful role in marginalising rather than amplifying teachers' voices' (160).

While these analyses are welcome, it is notable that they do not acknowledge how recent policy changes can be seen to be based, at least in part, in a perceived failure on the part of teachers to deliver what society required of them – arguably a failure of traditional professionalism. This view is reflected in the 'official' account of recent reform offered by Michael Barber, the key architect of New Labour's policies in England (e.g. Barber, 2005). He argues that there have been four phases of reform since the 1960s, as follows:

- *Uninformed professionalism* – the period prior to the 1980s, often regarded as the golden age of teacher autonomy but when, according to Barber, teachers lacked appropriate knowledge, skills and attitudes for a modern society.

- *Uninformed prescription* – the period following the election of Margaret Thatcher's Conservative Government in 1979 and, in particular, its imposition of a national curriculum in 1988 for political rather than educational reasons.

- *Informed prescription* – the period following the election of Tony Blair's New Labour Government in 1997, bringing with it (in Barber's view) 'evidence-based' policies such as the Literacy and Numeracy Strategies and Standards-based teacher training.

- *Informed professionalism* – a new phase, just beginning, when teachers will have the appropriate knowledge, skills and attitudes for the government to grant them a greater degree of licensed autonomy to manage their own affairs.

This account is itself not without difficulties. As Dainton (2005) rightly points out, it provides a crude analysis that is historically inaccurate, not least in relation to some real achievements during the first of these phases. She also wryly comments that 'delivering' someone else's thoughts, ideas, strategies and lesson plans hardly counts as 'informed professionalism' (159).

In response, however, I suggest in this paper that, while New Labour's managerialist reforms have so far failed to create the conditions for 'informed professionalism', let alone the positive equity outcomes that their advocates predicted, they have contained some 'progressive moments'. These will need to be held onto as we seek to develop new forms of professionalism that transcend both traditional professionalism and the attacks on that tradition implicit in recent reforms. I therefore interrogate these reforms with a view to establishing the possibilities for 'collaborative' and 'democratic' professionalisms. The distinction between these two emergent professionalisms has been developed subsequent to an earlier analysis (Whitty and Wisby, 2006) and produces a fourfold typology of teacher professionalisms – traditional, managerialist, collaborative and democratic.

Approaches to defining 'professionalism'

I begin by looking at approaches to defining 'professionalism'. Sociological discourse about professionalism and the state can go some way in helping us to understand the contemporary condition of teachers as professionals.

The nature of professionalism was initially subjected to concerted attention by Western sociologists in the 1950s. The main approach at this point focused on establishing the features that an occupation should have in order to be termed a profession. A typical list included such items as (Millerson, 1964):

- the use of skills based on theoretical knowledge

- education and training in those skills certified by examination

- a code of professional conduct oriented towards the 'public good'

- a powerful professional organisation.

These lists reflected the nature of established professions such as medicine and law, while occupations that did not entirely meet such criteria were given the title 'quasi-' or 'semi-professions' (Etzioni, 1969). Moving to 'full' professional status was seen as part of an aspiring occupation's 'professional project' and this has applied to the strategy of teachers in many countries.

In contrast, more recent sociological perspectives on professionalism have rejected such normative notions of what it means to be a professional. Instead, they see professionalism as a shifting phenomenon – a profession, they suggest, is whatever people think it is at any particular time (Hanlon, 1998). Rather than asking whether the teaching profession lives up to some supposed ideal, such an approach encourages us to explore the characteristics of teaching as an occupation in the present. Potentially, it also liberates us to conceptualise and work towards alternative conceptions of professionalism. Thus, it allows us to consider what might be appropriate 'prospective identities' for teachers in the current conjuncture (Bernstein, 1996).

In practice, of course, in most countries the characteristics of a profession have been increasingly determined by the state, which became the major stakeholder in defining professionalism in the twentieth century. Most professionals are now employed, or at least regulated, by governments. Professional status, therefore, is typically dependent on the sort of bargain an occupation has struck with the state – what is sometimes called its 'professional mandate'. The nature of teachers' professional mandate has become a key policy issue for governments in many countries, sometimes as part of a broader attempt to redefine professionalism, especially in the public sector, and sometimes as a specific aspect of education reform.

The extent to which national governments have been willing to intervene in teachers' work more directly – whether by prescribing the school curriculum and national systems of examination or, for example, through inspection – has varied between time and place. In many East Asian and continental European countries, there has traditionally been far more central control of some of these matters than in, say, England or the USA. Until recently, they have also been much more reluctant than the Anglo-Saxon countries to adopt marketisation as a means of educational reform. What seems to be happening now in many countries is a re-articulation of centralised policies with market-based ones to produce the apparent paradox of the 'free market and the strong state' or so-called 'quasi-markets', involving processes of centralised-decentralisation and 'steering at a distance' (Gamble, 1988).

The new right attack on traditional professionalism

The teaching profession in England has never enjoyed the 'licensed autonomy' that occupations such as medicine and law have traditionally had, whereby they have been permitted by the state to regulate their own affairs. Nevertheless, from the 1950s until the mid-1970s, it had experienced a considerable degree of de facto autonomy. Indeed, Le Grand (1997) has suggested that this period represented a golden age of teacher control. Parents were expected to trust teachers to know what was best for their children. Accordingly, the teacher's role included the freedom to decide not only how to teach but also what to teach. In this, they had a particular responsibility for curriculum development and innovation. Even though effectively the state paid most teachers' salaries, it did not intervene actively in the content of either teacher training or the work of teachers in schools.

From the mid-1970s, however, there were some dramatic changes in policy and, linked to these, attempts to change the nature of teacher professionalism. Due to economic downturn across the industrialised West, there was growing criticism of the 'swollen state' of post-war social democracy, not only for cost reasons but also because the welfare state had failed to deliver either efficiency or equity. Particularly under Thatcherism and similar regimes elsewhere, there were swingeing attacks on public-sector professions, including teachers, who were accused of abusing their autonomy to the detriment of pupils and society. This became coupled with an intellectual critique of public-sector management on the part of neo-liberals and public-choice theorists. The outcome was a call for public-sector providers to be subjected to greater accountability – both through market-based competition and increased surveillance by the state.

In England, the so-called 'liberal educational establishment', principally comprising teachers, the local authorities that employed them and the universities that trained them, came to be regarded by governments as left-leaning and favouring what in their view were highly questionable 'progressive' or 'child-centred' approaches to teaching. Together, lack of competitive discipline and 'progressive' teaching methods were blamed for a levelling down of standards. The effect of these attacks, whether deliberately or not, was to erode trust in teachers, thereby facilitating subsequent educational reform.

A key strand of policy, as in other countries, has been to re-position public-sector schools as competitors in the marketplace, encouraging them to behave more like those in the private sector. Parents have been offered greater choice over the school that their children attend, which is often coupled with a shift to per capita funding and, in some cases, experimental voucher systems. Budgets and managerial power are handed down to schools in the expectation that they can then respond more effectively to the preferences of parents as consumers.

However, while contemporary governments have been enthusiastic about making schools more receptive to parents' wishes, they are generally unwilling to relinquish control over the outcomes that schools should achieve. While devolution appears to offer organisations greater autonomy, the state retains overall strategic control by setting the outputs that providers need to achieve (Neave, 1988: 11), which in turn are operationalised through a range of targets and performance indicators. These have proliferated in recent years and in some countries, notably England, league tables have grown up around 'marketised' systems. Although often justified in terms of providing information for the 'consumer' and greater public accountability, the indicators also enable government to scrutinise and direct providers. Arguably, they also indirectly influence the priorities of parents – who in turn reinforce the pressure on schools to achieve government-determined outcomes (Adnett and Davies, 2003).

In England, the Conservative Government's 1988 Education Reform Act has often been seen as the epitome of a policy combining market forces and state control. The Act was not only significant in 'stepping-up' the process of marketisation; it was both substantive and symbolic in centralising power. This included granting 451 new powers directly to the Secretary of State for Education. It also included one of the most significant examples of centralisation under the Conservatives – the introduction of the National Curriculum and its associated national system of assessment.

The National Curriculum specified programmes of study and attainment targets for three 'core' subjects, English, mathematics and science (plus Welsh in Wales), and seven other 'foundation' subjects. This was intended to ensure that all students aged 5–16 followed a 'broad and balanced' curriculum. The curriculum was to be assessed by a complex system of national testing for pupils at ages 7, 11, 14 and 16. Whereas previously the content of lessons was largely, if not wholly, determined by individual schools or teachers, now it was a statutory requirement for teachers to follow the centrally prescribed curriculum. The national assessments generated a wealth of important data on school performance, thereby reinforcing the significance of the National Curriculum in shaping what teachers taught.

The developments I have outlined for England have obvious implications for teacher autonomy and teacher professionalism. Standardised criteria now feed into the framework of targets and indicators required of schools and individual teachers and the new assessment regimes provide a wealth of performance data for their managers at all levels of the system. Paradoxically, while apparently ceding more power to managers in schools, processes of 'steering at a distance' severely delimit and direct what and how they manage. Nevertheless, the stakes that are involved for schools have necessitated the growth of managerialism and the development of a distinct managerial tier within schools, one consequence of which is likely to be increased fragmentation of the profession.

At the same time as greater differentiation of roles within teaching, there have been different responses to recent education reforms. There appears to be an increasingly marked divide among teachers along the lines of what might be summarised as the 'new entrepreneurs' and 'old collectivists'. Those teachers who have enthusiastically adopted the changing agenda, and who are prepared to 'manage' on behalf of their employers, have gained enhanced status and rewards, including broader training opportunities and even a limited degree of licensed autonomy. By contrast, those pursuing the traditional welfarist agenda are no longer trusted and have to be controlled more directly through the detailed prescription and monitoring of their duties. The introduction of performance-related pay and fast-track training and career progression has compounded this divide.

New Labour's managerial professionalism

This managerialism was taken to new heights by the New Labour Government elected in 1997. Despite its proclaimed commitment to a 'Third Way', in practice its education reforms built on Margaret Thatcher's 'New Right settlement' and even went beyond it combining devolution, choice and even privatisation, on the one hand, and centralised regulation, monitoring and even pedagogical prescription on the other.

As part of this, however, the basic policy framework of 'quasi markets' has been harnessed to a much more explicit attempt to re-conceptualise and control teacher professionalism in accordance with New Labour's political project. While the Conservatives attempted to reduce the power of the teaching profession relative to other stakeholders, it still saw the individual teacher as the means of raising standards in schools. Under New Labour there has instead been a growing focus on education as a collective endeavour.

New Labour's approach is effectively summarised in the 1998 Green Paper, *Teachers: Meeting the Challenge of Change* (DfEE, 1998), which notes that 'the time has long gone when isolated, unaccountable professionals made curriculum and pedagogical decisions alone, without reference to the outside world' (14). It goes on to list what, in the Government's view, a modern teaching profession needs. This includes the call for teachers to:

- accept accountability

- seek to base decisions on evidence of what works in schools

- work in partnership with other staff in schools

- welcome the contribution that parents, business and others outside a school can make to its success.

There has thus been a reinforcement by New Labour of the need for the state to take a much more assertive role in specifying what teachers are expected to achieve, rather than leaving it to professional judgement alone. There is a real enthusiasm for intervening in the detail of educational processes, with advice on all aspects of the day-to-day running of schools and teaching itself. Furlong (2005) highlights the 2,000 model lesson plans that teachers can now download from the Government's website – something that would have been unthinkable in England not many years ago and is reminiscent of traditional English criticisms of highly centralised systems such as those of France and Japan.

The approach of intervening in the detailed processes of teaching, specifying how to teach in addition to what to teach, supposedly based on evidence of 'what works', is particularly evident in New Labour's National Strategies for Literacy and Numeracy – now subsumed into more broadly based Primary and Secondary Strategies. The Strategies have brought considerable funding for research and the production of classroom materials. Delivery has been standardised through prescribed content and training that promotes particular teaching approaches. This has been complemented by ambitious targets and a significant programme of pupil assessment to monitor achievement and the extent to which all pupils are reaching given levels of literacy and numeracy.

But the Strategies have had even wider implications for teachers in terms of the third element of the Green Paper – the need for teachers to work in partnership with other staff in schools, whose numbers have grown dramatically in recent years. Between 1997 and 2005 the number of teaching assistants in schools almost trebled – from 35,000 to just below 100,000. Over the same period the number of full-time equivalent (FTE) 'regular' teachers in the maintained sector reached 430,000. In the nursery and primary phases the number of FTE regular teachers actually dropped slightly to 196,000 (DfES, 2005).

There have also been marked changes in the nature of teaching assistants' responsibilities – with a shift in focus from 'care and housekeeping' to involvement in the actual process of learning and assessment of learning. Although the expansion of the number and role of teaching assistants is not a new idea in England (see Marland and Rutter, 2001), the Literacy and Numeracy Strategies were the main driver for change and the move of teaching assistants into learning support and teaching-type roles in mainstream classrooms. This has since been cemented by New Labour's workforce remodelling agenda.

One component of workforce remodelling has been the reallocation of various administrative and clerical duties from teachers to teaching assistants. This includes taking registers and low-level learning-related activities such as putting up displays, photocopying, record-keeping and invigilating. This role is obviously set below that of a teacher and implies working mainly under the supervision or guidance of the teacher.

Another component, however, has served to formalise a much expanded role for more experienced support staff. The Higher Level Teaching Assistant training and assessment programme, established in 2004, allowed teaching assistants to pursue 'higher level' status (see TTA, 2003). The role requires a trained person who carries out a range of tasks traditionally associated with teaching, including teaching classes under supervision. These teaching assistants still report to the teacher, but operate with a substantial degree of independence and creativity in their own right. They are clearly full participants in the processes of learning and teaching, and in the skills that underpin them, such as planning and evaluating pupils' progress (Kerry, 2005). This represents an important philosophical shift, namely that teachers' professional training, knowledge and experience prepare them to take overall responsibility for pupils' learning, but that they are not required to take sole responsibility for every aspect of each lesson that is taught (DfES/TTA, 2003: 4, cited in Kerry, 2005).

In this respect, the Government has played an active role in blurring the distinction between teachers and teaching assistants. Many of the teachers' unions have accepted this, albeit with varying degrees of enthusiasm, as a means of helping teachers to focus on teaching rather than administration or behaviour control. However, the largest teachers' union – The National Union of Teachers (NUT) – refused to support the policy. The union expressed concerns about declining standards where staff without a teaching qualification were left in charge of whole classes. So strong was its opposition, the union put full-page adverts in a national newspaper in an attempt to repel the initiative.

This rejection of the policy by the NUT could be seen as a very traditional professional strategy of exclusion in defence of its members' interests against New Labour's managerialist or 'managed' approach to teacher professionalism. By contrast, the Government presented the changes as being part of a process in which different professional and professionalising groups recognise their complementary roles in improving education in the interests of all (Morris, 2001). I would argue that, although the NUT's defensive, exclusory position is in some ways understandable – particularly in the face of government reforms that have undermined key elements of teachers' bargaining position – it is also likely to prove untenable and needs to be replaced with a more genuinely progressive strategy. This is particularly so if we look at other policy developments under New Labour.

For example, linked to workforce remodelling in schools is an even broader 'children's agenda', which encompasses the most radical changes in services for children and their families since the 1988 Children's Act (Reid, 2005). The central plank of this legislation – the 2004 Children Act – is based in a Green Paper entitled *Every Child Matters* (DfES, 2003), which was widely welcomed. It recognises the differential impact of home circumstances on children's achievement and requires schools to achieve five outcomes for all children, whatever their backgrounds. These are to 'be healthy, stay safe, enjoy and achieve, make a positive contribution and achieve economic well-being'.

To support these aims, the Act seeks to ensure multi-agency working in the interests of children. Accordingly, local authorities are being encouraged to bring together education and social services departments into powerful education and children's services departments and to establish 'children's trusts' to co-ordinate these services with other statutory and voluntary agencies. This will bring wide-ranging changes to the way in which different welfare services are configured, but also to the way both teaching and support staff work together and with other professionals.[1]

Collaborative professionalism

As family, community and children's welfare move alongside the traditional aims of education, schools will increasingly be involved in multi-agency working. As part of this, an 'extended schools' programme seeks to establish wider services in all primary and secondary schools – including study support and family learning opportunities and swift referral to a range of specialised support. There are also plans for increasing the number of 'full service extended schools', which will offer local communities access to courses and facilities, as well as services in childcare, youth justice, health and social care. This is something that has been tried successfully in Scotland and is seen as vital if the effects of social disadvantage on educational achievement are to be minimised (Sammons et al., 2002).

Such outcomes, and the inter- and multi-agency working that their realisation is likely to entail, obviously have significant implications for future professional training and continuing professional development needs. This will involve teachers working not as a largely separate professional group, but in active collaboration with other professionals, para-professionals and non-professionals from a range of possible disciplines. These include, among others, health visitors, general practitioners, social workers, education welfare officers, youth and community workers, education psychologists, speech and language therapists, learning mentors, the police and various local authority officers, as well as school support staff (see Reid, 2005).

Such moves will entail considerable cultural shifts on the parts of all the groups concerned. So far, it is still unclear how such teams will work together – or how the teaching profession specifically will choose to position itself within them. Some reflections on the part of Carol Adams, the first chief executive of the General Teaching Council for England (GTCE), illustrated the dilemma. While Adams herself welcomed many aspects of the children's agenda, she remained concerned that pupils, parents and the wider community could become confused about the unique contribution of the teacher. She also asked whether a child's right to learn could be threatened by the new multi-disciplinary agenda. In resisting the possibility that schools might become 'glorified social centres', she argued that we 'must hold fast to the simple premise that a school is a centre of learning' (Adams, 2005).

This idea resonated with other critiques of recent education reforms as likely to 'de-professionalise' teachers (e.g., Adams and Tulasiewicz, 1995; Tomlinson, 2001; Furlong, 2005). However, I would argue that, sociologically, it is not necessarily appropriate to view such developments as an example of de-professionalisation, but rather as an attempt at re-professionalisation – that is, the construction of a different type of professionalism, perhaps more appropriate to contemporary needs. Yet, even those commentators who move beyond critique to argue that teachers need to develop a more active and engaged professionalism and overcome traditional divisions within the teaching profession (e.g. Dainton, 2005; Leaton-Gray, 2006) do not go on to consider whether the boundaries between teacher professionalism and the professionalisms of other occupational groups themselves need to be questioned.

In my view, embracing collaborative professionalism is far preferable to seeking a return to traditional professionalism. Even though, in England, it has been initiated by managerialist reforms, it potentially offers teachers new professional opportunities to support children's learning by achieving a balance between defining the teacher's proper role and staking out the territory too rigidly. Identifying the contribution of teachers' specific expertise remains important, but this will need to be deployed and disseminated differently in collaborative contexts.

That said, our concern should not be merely to facilitate inter-professional working between distinct groups working in education or other services concerned with children and young people. Although teachers' organisations are now talking to organisations representing social workers, school nurses, health visitors and police officers about common aims, the case for common codes of conduct or statements of shared values and about shared training, this so far seems to be as much about staking out the territory for each profession more clearly, and thereby avoiding inter-professional rivalry, as it is about changing teachers' conventional ways of working in response to the new agenda.

While, as we have seen, some contemporary sociologists (e.g., Hanlon, 1998) have been content simply to move beyond normative understandings of what it means to be a professional, others, particularly those working in a feminist perspective, have taken a more directly critical stance. For example, Davies (1995, 1996) regards the 'old professions' as characterised by elitism, paternalism, control and detachment. This sociological critique of professionalism could equally apply to inter-professional agreements, where professions work with one another, but to the exclusion of other stakeholders.

We need to remember that part of the influence of the New Right reforms came from their appeal to voices within the wider community, including business and parents. Similar concerns informed one of the key principles of the 1998 New Labour Green Paper, which welcomed 'the contribution that parents, business and others outside a school can make to its success' (DfEE, 1988:120). All this suggests that we may need to move beyond even the collaborative form of professionalism and seek to establish what I and others have termed 'democratic professionalism' – a professionalism where teachers work in tandem with *all* relevant stakeholders (Whitty, 2002).

Towards a democratic professionalism

Democratic professionalism, then, involves being sensitive to a wide range of stakeholders, some of whose voices have traditionally been silent in education decision making (Apple, 1996). It seeks to demystify professional work and forge alliances between teachers and excluded constituencies of students, parents and members of the wider community, with a view to building a more democratic education system and ultimately a more open society.

Here too, it is possible to see that, ironically, the managerialist attack on traditional modes of teacher professionalism has opened up new possibilities. For example, in commenting on the increasing recognition of the importance of 'student voice' in school decision-making, Fielding (2004) notes:

> perhaps to our surprise, two decades of profoundly damaging policies and practices have also seen the emergence of apparently positive developments in what has come to be known as pupil or 'student voice'. As much as any development in schools in the last ten years, this 'new wave' of student voice activity seems to hold out real hope both for renewal and for the development of pre-figurative democratic practice that give teachers and students the courage and the

> confidence to create new practices and proposals for a more just and
> vibrant society.
>
> (Fielding, 2004: 198–9)

Similarly, government calls for increased influence by parents and business in schools potentially legitimate the involvement of other traditionally excluded constituencies in the wider community. In my view, democratic professionalism requires not merely much stronger professional associations, whether of teachers or the wider children's workforce, but much more active engagement with a wide range of stakeholders committed to a just society (Gale and Densmore, 2000, 2003). Sachs' (2003) notion of the 'activist identity' for teachers goes some way towards recognising this. Her activist professional works collectively towards strategic ends, operates on the basis of developing networks and alliances between bureaucracies, unions, professional associations and community organisations. These alliances are not static, but form and are re-formed around different issues and concerns. Activist professionals take responsibility for their own ongoing professional learning, and work within communities of practice, which develop in larger contexts – historical, social, cultural and institutional (Sachs, 2001).

This requires teachers to conceive of themselves as 'agents of change' rather than 'victims of change' (Johnson and Hallgarten, 2002), something that will not be easy in England, not least because recent policies have undermined both the morale of, and public trust in, the teaching workforce. This, in turn, has limited the extent to which teachers can engage authoritatively with other stakeholders. Nevertheless, if they are committed to fostering social justice, teachers and their professional associations will need to work with others to grasp and help shape the progressive opportunities that are provided by policies such as those relating to workforce remodelling and the children's agenda.

Lewis (forthcoming) has recently argued that a 'new professionalism' is not a new professionalism unless it is 'enacted' by practising professionals. She criticises what I have called 'managerial professionalism' as 'demanded' or 'prescribed' rather than enacted in her sense. Clearly neither 'collaborative' nor 'democratic' professionalism are as yet sufficiently enacted, but I would argue that they do have greater potential than 'managerial' professionalism to be embraced and enacted by practising professionals.

Leaton-Gray (2006) has rightly claimed that the restriction of teachers' professional autonomy by recent managerialist reforms has sometimes 'undermined teachers as educators and their pupils as learners' (178). However, these emergent forms of professional engagement and their associated professional identities provide much greater hope of empowering teachers and pupils for a democratic future than those offered by traditional notions of teacher autonomy and a traditional model of professionalism. In my view, both collaborative and democratic professionalisms are potentially progressive modes of professionalism that could still emerge from recent education reforms.

Acknowledgements

I am grateful to Emma Wisby and Sarah Tough for their help in developing this chapter. An earlier version, 'Teacher professionalism in a new era', was presented as the first General Teaching Council for Northern Ireland Annual Lecture, Belfast, March 2006 and was developed as an article entitled '"Collaborative" and "democratic" professionalisms: alternatives to "traditional" and "managerialist" approaches to teacher autonomy?', which appeared in *Educational Studies in Japan: International Yearbook,* No. 1, 2006, 25–36.

References

Adams, A. and Tulasiewicz, W. (1995) *The Crisis in Teacher Education: A European concern?* London: Falmer Press.

Adams, C. (2005) Comments made at the Institute of Ideas 'Battle of Ideas' Conference, 29–30 October.

Adnett, N. and Davies, P. (2003) 'Schooling reforms in England: From quasi-markets to co-opetition?' *Journal of Education Policy*, 18 (4): 393–406.

Apple, M. (1996) *Cultural Politics and Education*. Buckingham: Open University Press.

Barber, M. (2005) 'Informed professionalism: realising the potential'. Presentation to a conference of the Association of Teachers and Lecturers, London, 11 June.

Bernstein, B. (1996) *Pedagogy, Symbolic Control and Identity: Theory, research, critique*. Oxford: Rowman & Littlefield.

Dainton, S. (2005) 'Reclaiming teachers' voices'. *Forum*, 47 (2): 159–67.

Davies, C. (1995) *Gender and the Professional Predicament in Nursing*. Buckingham: Open University Press.

Davies, C. (1996) 'The sociology of professions and the profession of gender'. *Sociology*, 30: 661–78.

DfEE [Department for Education and Employment] (1998) *Teachers: Meeting the Challenge of Change*. Green Paper. London: DfEE.

DfES [Department for Education and Skills] (2003) *Every Child Matters: Change for Children*. London: DfES.

DfES (2005) *School Workforce in England*. January (provisional). Online <http://www.dfes.gov.uk/rsgateway/DB/SFR/s000575/index.shtml> (accessed 7 January 2008).

Etzioni, A. (ed.) (1969), *The Semi-Professions and their Organisation: Teachers, nurses, social workers*. London: Collier-Macmillan.

Fielding, M. (1999) 'Radical collegiality: affirming teaching as an inclusive professional practice'. *Australian Educational Researcher*, 26 (2): 1–34.

Fielding, M. (2004) '"New wave" student voice and the renewal of civic society'. *London Review of Education*, 2 (3): 197–216.

Furlong, J. (2005) 'New Labour and teacher education: the end of an era'. *Oxford Review of Education*, 31 (1): 119–34.

Gamble, A. (1988) *The Free Economy and the Strong State*. London: Macmillan.

Gale, T. and Densmore, K. (2000) *Just Schooling: Explorations in the Cultural Politics of Teaching*. Buckingham: Open University Press.

Gale, T. and Densmore, K. (2003) *Engaging Teachers: Towards a Radical Democratic Agenda for Schooling*. Maidenhead: Open University Press.

Hanlon, G. (1998) 'Professionalism as enterprise: service class politics and the redefinition of professionalism'. *Sociology*, 32: 42–63.

Helsby, G. and McCulloch, G. (1996) 'Teacher Professionalism and Curriculum Control'. In I.F. Goodson and A. Hargreaves (eds), *Teachers' Professional Lives*. London: Falmer Press.

Johnson, M. and Hallgarten, J. (eds) (2002), *From Victims of Change to Agents of Change: The future of the teaching profession*. London: Institute for Public Policy Research.

Kerry, T. (2005) 'Towards a typology for conceptualizing the roles of teaching assistants'. *Educational Review*, 57 (3): 373–84.

Lawton, D. (1980) *The Politics of the School Curriculum*. London: Routledge & Kegan Paul.

Le Grand, J. (1997) 'Knights, knaves or pawns? Human behaviour and social policy'. *Journal of Social Policy*, 26: 149–64.

Leaton Gray, S. (2006) *Teachers Under Siege*. Stoke-on-Trent: Trentham Books.

Lewis, L. (forthcoming) 'Professionalism, professionality and the development of education professionals'. *British Journal of Educational Studies*.

Marland, M. and Rutter, A. (2001) 'Unsung heroes'. *Report – magazine of the Association of Teachers & Lecturers*, 24 (2): 11.

Millerson, G. (1964) *The Qualifying Association*. London: Routledge & Kegan Paul.

Morris, E. (2001) *Professionalism and Trust: The Future of Teachers and Teaching*. London: DfES/Social Market Foundation.

Neave, G. (1988) 'On the cultivation of quality, efficiency and enterprise: an overview of recent trends in higher education in Western Europe, 1968–1998'. *European Journal of Education*, 23 (1/2): 7–23.

Reid, K. (2005) 'The implications of Every Child Matters and the Children Act for schools'. *Pastoral Care*, March, 12–18.

Sachs, J. (2001) 'Teacher professional identity: competing discourses, competing outcomes'. *Journal of Education Policy*, 16 (2): 149–61.

Sachs, J. (2003) 'Teacher professional standards: controlling or developing teaching?' *Teachers & Teaching: Theory and Practice*, 9 (2): 175–86.

Sammons, P., Power, S., Robertson, P., Elliot, K., Campbell, C. and Whitty, G. (2002) *Interchange 76: National Evaluation of the New Community Schools Pilot Programme in Scotland: Phase 1: Interim Findings*. Edinburgh, Scottish Executive.

TTA [Teacher Training Agency] (2003) *Professional Standards for Higher Level Teaching Assistants*. Online. <http://www.tda.gov.uk/upload/resources/pdf/h/hlta-standards-v6.pdf.> (accessed 23 November 2007).

Tomlinson, S. (2001) *Education in a Post-Welfare Society*. Buckingham: Open University Press.

Whitty, G. (2002) *Making Sense of Education Policy*. London: Sage.

Whitty, G. and Wisby, E. (2006) 'Moving beyond recent education reform – and towards a democratic professionalism'. *Hitotsubashi Journal of Social Studies*, 38 (1): 43–61.

Note

1 The Government's *Children's Plan*, setting out the Government's ten-year 'vision' for children, was being published as this chapter went to press.

4 Performativity, privatisation, professionals and the state
Stephen J. Ball[1]

In this paper I want to discuss and to join up three different aspects of education policy on which I have been doing work over the past few years. These are: (i) performativity, that is a technology and a mode of regulation that employs judgements, comparisons and displays as measures of productivity or output or value of individuals and organisations; (ii) privatisation, that is the use of the 'market form' to reform public-sector institutions (endogenous privatisation) or private providers to deliver state education services (exogenous privatisation); and (iii) changes in the form and modalities of the state, a move from *government* (bureaucracy and administration) to *governance* (enterprise and networks). At the centre of this infrastructure of policy and these processes of change, I place the teacher[2] – the education professional – as a subject of reform. I will range widely across three different literatures and, importantly, I write from a subject position inside this intersection of the incitements and seductions of reform.

What I am going to argue is that the inter-relations among these different policy moves address, require and enable the reform of the teacher and are profoundly changing teaching and the meaning of professionalism and what it means to be a teacher. These policies do not just change the ways teachers work and how they are employed and paid, they also change who they are, how we judge them and how we define a good teacher. In other words, they require us to work on ourselves and to become 'self-aware' in particular ways. They produce a new repertoire of possibilities of being, while excluding or residualising others.

A clear presentation of these policy moves and their inter-relationships is not going to be easy; each is embedded in the other and the inter-relationships are multi-faceted and complex. Together they are creating a new episteme of public service through a 'reshaping of "deep" social relations' (Leys, 2001: 2) which involve the subordination of moral obligations to economic ones (Walzer, 1984) so that 'everything is simply a sum of value realised or hoped for' (Slater and Tonkiss, 2001: 142). Productive individuals, new kinds of subjects, are the central resource in a reformed, entrepreneurial public sector. Let me begin by explaining further and illustrating each of the components before I consider how they impinge upon the lives and persons and work of teachers.

Performativity

Performativity is a term that is increasingly widely used in policy analysis writing, but it is not always used in its full sense. What I mean by that is that the usefulness of the concept is not just as another way of referring to systems of performance management, but it alludes to the work that performance management systems do on the subjectivities of individuals. Performativity invites and incites us to make ourselves more effective, to work on ourselves to improve ourselves and to feel guilty or inadequate if we do not. But it operates within a framework of judgement within which what improvement is is determined for us, and 'indicated' by measures of quality and productivity. Performativity is enacted through measures and targets against which we are expected to position ourselves, but often in ways that also produce uncertainties about how we should organise ourselves within our work. Shore and Wright (1999) even go so far as to suggest that these uncertainties are a tactic of destabilisation. Performativity 'works' most powerfully when it is inside our heads and our souls. That is, when we do it to ourselves, when we take responsibility for working hard, faster and better as part of our sense of personal worth and the worth of others. And it is important to recognise that it also offers us the possibility of being better than we were or even being the best – better than others. We can become recognised as competent, marketable and desirable and accrue to ourselves the rewards of being culturally intelligible subjects. Performativity is not in any simple sense a technology of oppressions, it is also one of satisfactions and rewards, at least for some. Indeed it works best when we come to want for ourselves what is wanted from us, when our moral sense of ourselves and our desires are aligned with the pleasures of performativity. But there is always the possibility of slippage between pleasure and tyranny within performativity regimes. Experienced either way its effects are to alter our working practices, our goals and satisfactions *and our identities* – our sense of who we are at work. In a sense it is about making the individual into an enterprise, a self-maximising productive unit operating in a market of performances – a 'headlong pursuit of relevance as defined by the market' (Falk, 1999).

Within all this the organisation – school, college, university or agency – and the person are treated in exactly the same way. The self-managing individual and the autonomous organisation are produced within the interstices of performativity through audits, inspections, appraisals, self-reviews, quality assurance, research assessments, etc. We and our workplace are made visible and we become 'subjects which have to be seen' (Foucault, 1979: 187). These techniques and devices taken as a whole constitute a political economy of details, 'small acts of cunning' (139) that work as mundane but inescapable technologies of 'modernisation' and 'transformation' which, acting across the whole public sector, produce a dense web of power relations. Audits of various sorts work 'both to evaluate and to shape the performance of the auditee in three dimensions: economy, efficiency and effectiveness' (Power, 1994: 34). But again the effectiveness of the audit, its shaping of action, arises from the extent to which it is taken seriously and internalised by actors as something they do to themselves, as ways in which we represent ourselves and what we do. In being responsible and serious we make our work and ourselves into measurable entities and render our worth in terms of our 'output'. The processes of education are reified and raised to 'a state of perpetual self-awareness, animation and explicitness' (Strathern, 1997: 318). Ofsted inspections can now take place with just 24 hours' notice! That which cannot be made explicit in this sense is in danger of becoming redundant. Performativity colonises all aspects of practice and requires us to be constantly reflexive and self-disciplining, weighing up the costs and benefits of our actions in terms of their investment in productive outcomes, the imperative to do more and be more, and thus it drives out those things that cannot be justified in its terms. One of the victims of this kind of calculation is sociability – guilt and self-dissatisfaction and the continuous demand that we add value to ourselves mean that more time is spent at the computer with a sandwich for lunch so that time is not 'wasted' – or changes in the form of sociability; a move to what Wittel calls 'network sociality' which is 'informational' rather than narrational, and based on the exchange of data. Here social relations themselves are a commodity – something to be 'invested in', that produces 'returns'. As Wittel (2001: 71) puts it, 'the paradigmatic form of late capitalism and the new cultural economy' is 'characterised by the assimilation of work and play ... [and the] increasing commodification and the increasing perception of social relationships as social capital'. In effect, in Wittel's terms, we no longer simply *have* social relationships, we *do* them, and such relationships have to be *managed*. Others are valued in terms of their performative worth and those who 'under-perform' are subject to moral approbation. Systems designed to 'support' or encourage those who are unable to 'keep up' continuously teeter on the brink of moral regulation.

Another consequence of continual animation and calculation is for many a growing sense of ontological insecurity: both a loss of a sense of meaning in what we do and of what is important in what we do. Are we doing things for the 'right' reasons – and how can we know? The first-order effect of performativity is to re-orient pedagogical and scholarly activities towards those that are likely to have a positive impact on measurable performance outcomes and such a deflection of attention away from aspects of social, emotional or moral development that have no immediate measurable performative value. Teachers' judgements about class or lecture room processes may thus be subverted and superseded by the demands of measurement, or at the very least a new set of dilemmas is produced which sets the tyranny of metrics over and against professional judgement. These include procedures such as quality assurance in higher education (Morley, 2003), the Research Assessment Exercise (Broadhead and Howard, 1998), and the 'necessities' involved in 'self' evaluation of schools for Ofsted.

A second-order effect is that for many teachers this changes the way in which they experience their work and the satisfactions they get from it – their sense of moral purpose and of responsibility for their students is distorted. Practice can come to be experienced as inauthentic and alienating. Commitments are sacrificed for impression. But the force and logic of performance are hard to avoid. To do so, in one sense at least, means letting ourselves down, and letting down our colleagues and our institution. Social structures and social relations are replaced by informational structures. We are burdened with the responsibility to perform, and if we do not we are in danger of being seen as irresponsible. Performativity is a moral system that subverts and re-orients us to its ends. 'There are two technologies at play here turning us into governable subjects – a technology of *agency* and a technology of *performance*' (Davies and Petersen, 2005: 93). We are produced rather than oppressed, animated rather than constrained!

In all of this the meaning of professionalism, the idea of 'being professional' is re-worked and re-oriented, both in terms of goals and commitments. Perryman (2006) describes this in her case study of Northgate School as a process of 'deprofessionalisation'. This is 'the re-invention of professionals themselves as units of resource whose performance and productivity must constantly be audited so that it can be enhanced' (Shore and Wright, 1999: 559). We are re-made as units of resource, and activity, within 'the knowledge economy' and are enrolled into the processes of what is sometimes called '360 degree evaluation' – of everyone by everyone. These are the new spaces and the new visibilities within which we relate to one another, and seek our place and our worth and our needs. That is, 'the technology of statistics creates the capacity to relate to reality as a field of government' (Hunter, 1996: 154).

Regimes of performativity also generate new kinds of work and indeed there are new performative professions that rely on the 'authority and apparent objectivity of disciplines such as accountancy, economics and management' (MacKinnon, 2000: 297) – who in Weber's terms are 'specialists without spirit'. Mahony *et al.* (2004a) argue that the application of such specialist knowledge to teaching involves a process of 'masculinisation'. Measurement requires that data are collected and collated and filed and reported, all of which costs time and money – the transaction costs of performativity.

Dear Stephen,

Where outputs are included in the Institute's RAE submission which draw on research funded by the Research Councils (that is, ESRC, AHRC/AHRB, MRC or EPSRC), we would like to refer in the text box to the grade that was awarded by the Research Council to the final report for the project. For example:

'The research draws on an ESRC-funded project, part of the [title] Programme, which was graded outstanding.'

Three of the outputs, which we are including for you, are described as drawing on one or more Research Council-funded projects, but we do not have a record of the grade given to the final report. Please would you therefore, as a matter of urgency, provide the following information: ...

We are required to spend increasing amounts of our time in making ourselves accountable, reporting on what we do rather than doing it. And there is a particular set of skills to be acquired here – skills of presentation and of inflation, making the most of ourselves, making a spectacle of ourselves. We become transparent but empty, unrecognisable to ourselves – 'I am other to myself precisely at the place where I expect to be myself' (Butler, 2004: 15).

The point is that we make ourselves calculable rather than memorable. Experience is nothing, productivity is everything. We must keep up, meet the new and ever more diverse targets which we set for ourselves in appraisal meetings, confess and confront our weaknesses, undertake appropriate and value-enhancing professional development, and take up opportunities for making ourselves more productive, ensuring what O'Flynn and Petersen (2007: 469) call a 'targeted self' or what Gee (1999) refers to as the 'shape-shifting portfolio person'. Within all of this more and more of the personality is rendered explicit and auditable.

All of this can take its toll. Performativity comes to be inscribed on our bodies as well as our minds, making us anxious, tired and stressed and sometimes ill – like Sparkes' (2007) fictional academic Jim, and Canaan's (2008) account of Susan's experience of a university sickness policy and the ways in which 'some kinds of lecturers' bodies are now being deemed "abject" as they apparently function (or malfunction) in ways that others do not' (and see also Health Sociology Review, 2005).

> After the three hour meeting (to discuss the publications of his departmental staff with his vice chancellor), Jim was drained, empty. As he walked back to his office he went through a range of emotions – anger, disappointment, fear, helplessness. Confusion, shame, insecurity, anxiety, determination, hostility. There was also a little bit of pride for a job 'well done', in that he had managed to get most of his staff successfully through the process for another year. But then he felt complicit, tainted by management speak and their business world ideology. He had played the game on *their* terms, not his. He had played a game he did not believe in. He played a game that made him despair and feel sick inside.
>
> (Sparkes, 2007: 528)

Jim works 60 hours a week and drinks too much. His GP refers him to a consultant psychiatrist who reflects that 'In the past five years what began as a trickle of university teachers referred to him by their general practitioners was fast becoming a torrent' (536). Jim's sense of helplessness arises in part from his attempt to live up to and manage 'the contradictions of belief and expectation' (Acker and Feuerverger, 1997; quoted in Dillabough, 1999: 382) without any recourse to others. In Bauman's (1991: 197) terms this is 'the privatisation of ambivalence'. Performativity individualises and fragments and leaves us to struggle alone with our doubts and fears.

Privatisation

I now want to say something about a second dimension of contemporary education policy which impinges directly and indirectly on our practice – privatisation. Privatisation comes in many varieties and affects many different aspects of public service education, but I want to separate out two different forms which are invested in policy. First is 'endogenous' privatisation, that is, the importing of ideas, techniques and practices from the private sector in order to make the public sector more like businesses and more businesslike. These would include things like choice, budget devolution, competition, new managerialism, contract and competitive funding, performance management, and enterprise. Second is 'exogenous' privatisation, which involves the opening up of public education services to private sector participation on a for-profit basis and using the private sector to design, manage or deliver aspects of public education. This also extends to the privatisation of policy programmes and of policy itself through advice, consultancy, evaluations and research, and policy formulation and writing (see Ball, 2007a).

The key point I want to make here concerns the relationships that exist between privatisation and performativity. One part of what performativity does, as outlined above, is to re-render practice into measurable outcomes. That is, the work, the processes, of education come to be represented and appreciated in terms of products, or calculabilities. Individuals and institutions are required to account for themselves in ways that represent education as a standardised and measurable product as a basis for judgement and comparison. Insofar as this happens then a number of other things become possible:

- Individuals and institutions can be managed through the use of targets and benchmarks.

- Individuals and institutions can be rewarded, differentially, in relation to their productivity or in response to target achievements. At the individual level this can be translated into systems of performance-related-pay, and bonus or incentive schemes (Mahony *et al.*, 2004b). This is 'the re-invention of professionals themselves as units of resource whose performance and productivity must constantly be audited so that it can be enhanced' (Shore and Wright, 1999: 559).

- Also at an individual level, employees can be contracted on the basis of output requirements. This enables greater use of fixed-term contracts and individual contract negotiations and thus provides for greater budgetary flexibility.

- At the institutional level the work of the organisation as a whole can be rendered into performance indicators and again can be translated into the form of a contract for 'service delivery'.

- Once rendered into the form of such a contract, the work of organisations can be put out to tender on a fixed-cost, performance-related basis, and opened up to new providers – it can be exogenously privatised!

> Academies run by a high-profile sponsor are asking staff to sign contracts giving them tougher conditions, including halving the amount of paid maternity leave. The National Union of Teachers in Southwark, south London, is urging members not to sign contracts at academies sponsored by the charity Ark (Absolute Return for Kids). It has also criticised contracts introduced at academies sponsored by Carpetright entrepreneur Lord Harris of Peckham. Southwark is becoming increasingly dominated by academies. By 2009, there will be eight in the borough out of a total 16 secondaries. There is already only one community school. A comparison of Ark academy policy and the standard school contracts, shown to the NUT, suggests the length of maternity leave on full pay has been more than halved from nine to four weeks. Teachers are subject to a six-month probationary period and written warnings remain live on file for twice as long. They are required to work around five extra days a year.
>
> (Barker, 2007)

Contract is an increasingly important administrative and regulatory instrument. Contracting 'refers to a process whereby a government procures education or education-related services, of a defined volume and quantity, at an agreed price, from a specific provider for a specified period where the provisions between the financier and the service provider are recorded in contract' (Patrinos, 2005: 2–3). In education there is already a wide variety of such contracts in operation – what is commonly called 'outsourcing'. The majority of these apply to the provision of 'hard' services like catering, cleaning, maintenance, connectivity, security, back-office work, etc. but there are also many examples of 'soft' services that are outsourced. Part of 14 local education authorities have been contracted out to private providers and two local authority Children's Services divisions. These contracts normally arise from serious concerns about local authorities' performance and capacity identified in Ofsted inspections (see Campbell *et al.* (2004) and subsequent 'recommendations' made by consultants (PriceWaterhouseCoopers in many cases) to the (then) DfES and negotiations between local authorities and the DfES about appropriate remedial action. Consultants also write the contracts on which the outsourcing is based and act as 'brokers' in advising the local authorities concerned on the award of the contract. In addition, four English state schools (three of them in Surrey) have been contracted out to private companies; two are run by a company called 3Es, which was recently acquired by GEMS – a Dubai-based education and health management company, which also recently bought a chain of English private schools. Another contracted-out school in England was run by Nord-Anglia. The most recent example, which came into operation in September 2007, is a three-year contract to run Salisbury School in Enfield awarded to EdisonschoolsUK, a subsidiary of the US Edison Corporation. Part of the company's payment will be based on pupils achieving better GCSE grades and scores in national tests for 14-year-olds. The management team is being led by Trevor Averre-Beeson, a former head of Islington Green School in north London. In 2003 Edison ran one-quarter of the 417 contracted-out schools in the US, teaching 132,000 students in 20 states (see Saltman, 2005). Here profit is exacted from the difference, if one can be achieved, between the contract funding and the costs of delivery.

> BREAK them up and sell the bits to the highest bidder. That's the
> government's plan for some 44 research establishments funded by the
> public sector. So a dark shadow hovers over organisations like the
> British Geological Survey, the Institute of Food Research and the
> Transport Research Laboratory ... As the general election approaches,
> I predict that we shall hear a great deal more about the damaging
> effects of what the IPMS calls 'the contract culture'. And the clamor
> will come not just from the scientists employed by the research
> establishments involved, but from local communities where the
> establishments are the largest employer. The National Physical
> Laboratory is for example the largest employer in Teddington.
>
> (Dalyell, 1997)

However, we cannot assume that contracts always work or work as intended, as Gray (1997) illustrates in her discussion of the performance management of Training and Enterprise Councils. Her examples show 'how the preoccupation with quantitative indicators and quantitative targets in 'contract culture' leads to perverse results' (353). She calls these perversities *'target fetishism'*, that is 'a concern with targets which threatens to become detached from the social purposes of the policies at stake' (353). A rather tragic example is evident in the US health system – the publication of surgeons' morbidity rates, as a measure of quality and a source of information for clients, has led to a situation in which some patients find it difficult to find a surgeon to operate on them because they are 'high risk'. In effect, those who are most ill find it most difficult to get treatment. Fetishism can also spill over into 'opportunistic' behaviours and performance inflation.

> In addition to charges that Edison manipulated test reporting, it has
> been accused of encouraging cheating on tests in classrooms. This
> scandal erupted in the winter of 2002 when the Wichita Eagle reported
> that, in interviews with seven former Edison teachers, four of the
> seven said that they had been told by the company 'to do whatever it
> took to make sure students succeeded on standardized tests, including
> ignoring time limits, reading questions from a reading comprehension
> test aloud and in some cases correcting answers during a test.'
>
> (Saltman, 2005: 73–4)

Contracts bring about a reshaping of the culture and structures of governance and of service relationships and of the commitments of public service workers. At heart, this is a process of disaggregation and individualisation both of governance itself and of service relationships which are increasingly 'conceived as a series of cascading contracts linking principals and agents' (Yeatman, 1996: 285). Collectivist conceptions of 'genuinely public values' (Yeatman, 1996) are displaced. The social contract within which the professional works in the public interest is replaced by commercial relationships between educator and client and employer. There is an 'abandonment of any idea of the body politic' (Yeatman, 1996: 287) – and yet it is only in relationship to this idea that state professionalism makes sense. The body politic is replaced by what Foucault (1979: 194) calls 'mercantile society', which 'is represented as a contractual association of isolated juridical subjects'. This is, as Vincent-Jones (2006) argues, a distinctive new mode of governance. Contracts, he suggests, take three main forms – administrative, economic and social control – and 'each entails the deliberate attempt by the state to structure social behaviour ... through regulatory arrangements that harness the contract norms for the attainment of determinate public policy purposes' (vii–viii).

Contractualism and juridical forms are also being extended to the educational process. This is the precondition of the knowledge economy, or what Lyotard (1984) calls 'the mercantilization of knowledge' (51). Knowledge is no longer legitimated through 'grand narratives of speculation and emancipation' (38) but, rather, in the pragmatics of 'optimization' – the creation of skills or of profit rather than ideals. This is summed up, in Lyotard's terms, in a shift from the questions 'is it true?' and 'is it just?' to 'is it useful, saleable, efficient?'. And what is to count as worthwhile knowledge is determined by the user. Furthermore, the 'mercantile paradigm', as O'Sullivan (2005: 230) calls it, 'in its constitution and construction, it instrumentalises solidarity and then works to erode it wherever it might persist'.

Again then there are both practical and moral changes involved in these privatisations. Privatisation reforms change what is important and valuable and necessary in education, and as a new policy paradigm the market form constitutes a new moral environment for both consumers and producers. Within this new moral environment, schools, colleges and universities – their staff and their students – are being inducted into a 'culture of self interest' (cf. Morley 2003). For staff, self-interest is manifest in terms of survivalism, that is, an increased, often predominant, orientation towards the internal well-being of the institution and its members and a shift away from concern with more general social and educational issues within 'the community'. Saltman (2000) sees the hegemony of the market and the profit incentive as displacing the struggle over values, which is an essential condition of democracy. What we are seeing here is a kind of collapse of the boundaries between moral spheres, which follows the breakdown of the demarcations between public and private provision and between social and opportunity goods.

The private sector is now embedded in the heart and sinews of state education services at all levels, intertwined in the day-to-day business of decision making, infrastructural development, capacity building and service delivery (Ball, 2007b). Privatisation is now embedded in the heart and sinews of state education institutions as performativity, competition, choice, enterprise and budget-maximising behaviours insinuate themselves into everyday practice.

The state

The final element in this set of relationships and inter-relationships between agencies, actors and processes of reform is the state. That is, changes within public-sector institutions and the participation of private providers in public-sector delivery and policy are related to, and are part of, more general changes in the form and modalities of the state – what it looks like and how it works. In the simplest sense, the more the state contracts (out) the more it *contracts* (the central bureaucracies of the state reduce in size). As a result, policy processes occur in spaces parallel to and across state institutions and their jurisdictional boundaries – involving agencies, partnerships, consultants and contracted services. This is a move towards a polycentric state – a shift that is from government to governance and 'a shift in the centre of gravity around which policy cycles move' (Jessop, 1998: 32). There is a catalysing of public, private and voluntary actors to solve social and community problems, and resultant changes in the boundary between state and civil society. A new form of 'experimental' and 'strategic' governance is being fostered, based upon network relations within new policy communities. This entails a move away from state control to 'state steering' (Zambeta, 2002) as the means of managing and co-ordinating state functions. It is by no means a total move from one to the other, not a giving up of control, but the deployment of different kinds of mechanisms of power in at least some fields of activity. As Newman (2001: 30) explains, governance is 'a complex contested domain: one in which multiple forms of knowledge and power interact, and in which multiple narratives, assumptions and expectations shape social action and guide decision-making'. The state is by no means impotent in all this, but is now dependent upon an extensive array of state and non-state policy actors to achieve its ends. This does not involve a giving-up by the state of its capacity to drive and co-ordinate policy, this is not a 'hollowing out' of the state; rather it is a new modality of state power, agency and social action and indeed a new form of state. Specifically, what some writers have called the 'institutional void' created by the dissolution of administrative systems has been filled by systems of performativity and accountability which frame, regulate and orient the new 'autonomies' granted to policy agencies. This produces contradictory movements of centralisation and decentralisation. Governance takes the form of 'centres of calculation'

– acting at a distance – 'key nodes where information is compared, combined and aggregated' (Latour, 1987: 237–40). This produces a situation that Bernstein (1996: 12) calls 'decentred centralism' and that Richards and Smith (2002: 28–36) call a 'post-modern state', which is made up of what Kickert *et al.* (1997) refer to as 'loosely-coupled weakly-tied multi-organisational sets', and which is dependent, flexible, reflexive and diffuse but centrally steered. Policy is being 'done' in a multiplicity of new sites 'tied together on the basis of alliance and the pursuit of economic and social outcomes' (MacKenzie and Lucio, 2005: 500). While steering may become more complicated across the 'tangled web' of policy networks, the 'core executive' retains a substantial authoritative and co-ordinating presence over policy (Marinetto, 2003) and in some respects, and certainly in education, has achieved an enhancement of 'capacity of the state to project its influence and secure its objectives by mobilizing knowledge and power resources from influential non-governmental partners and stakeholders' (Jessop, 2002: 206).

This new mode of governance works both on the structures and content of public-sector institutions. They embody and sponsor, scaffold and disseminate the twin narratives of managerialism and enterprise – which are drawn from and 'sold' (through advice and consultancy and 'improvement programmes') by the private sector (see Ball, 2007b). New governance is both discursive and strategic and while discourse exists at an abstract level it has the ability to arrange and rearrange, form and re-form, position and identify whatsoever and whomsoever exists within its field. It has a 'heavy and fearsome materiality'. Bureau-professional regimes are displaced by regimes of enterprise. Professional 'enclosures' of specialist knowledge are breached, and professionalism is displaced from its 'precarious, glittering existence'. Or rather, perhaps there is produced a 'new' professionalism, what Rose (1996: 55) describes as a 'reconfiguration of the political salience of expertise, a new way of "responsibilizing" experts in relation to claims upon them other than those of their own criteria of truth and competence', the arts and skills of entrepreneurism being one form of new responsibility. To the extent that this new responsibility is taken seriously, the social, political and economic goals of the state are reproduced within the commitments, choices and obligations – the conduct that is – of individual actors within public-sector institutions. These 'new' professionals act prudentially and innovatively to protect and further the interests of their organisation – to achieve targets, to maximise income and to compete effectively within the new market-like mechanisms which encourage state institutions to compete with one another.

Management and enterprise are also a means of interjecting practical innovations and new sensibilities into areas of education policy that are seen as change-resistant and risk-averse. And, more generally, they 'pilot' and disseminate as 'good practice' the conditions (strategic and discursive) for a 'post-welfare' education system in which the state contracts and monitors, but does not deliver, education services – thus creating new opportunities for profit for the private sector. Through its deployment of the technologies of performance management and the market, the state acts as a 'commodifying agent', both rendering education into commodity and contractable forms, and 'recalibrating institutions' to make them homological with the firm and creating the necessary economic and extra-economic conditions within the public sector within which business can operate.

Teachers – subject to reform

The concatenation of processes of change outlined here involves, as I have tried to stress, not simply a set of structural and technical changes in public service delivery but also potentially profound changes in the meaning of work in the public sector and to the subjectivities of public-sector workers; although, in fact, a whole variety of new subject positions are interpolated within these changes. Crucially, for workers like teachers, as Rose (1996: 56) points out, this involves 'the supplanting of certain norms, such as those of service and dedication, with others such as those of competition, quality and customer demand'. We are re-positioned as 'autonomous' but 'calculating' agents. We are thus made responsive and productive. Deliberation and judgement are no longer of value here – except when applied to commercial well-being. Our contractual obligations, survival in the marketplace or achievement of targets are the new basis of 'professional' responsibility. In practice, however, things are not that clear-cut. The old and new professionalisms crash and grate, within and between individual actors. At an individual level we are mostly left to struggle with the difficult dilemmas involving organisational self-interests being set over and against obligations to our students and 'old' commitments like equity and fairness and scholarship. Such struggles can be stressful and debilitating and take their toll on mental and physical well-being, as Perryman (2007) documents. For some the inability to reconcile these different forms of responsibility leads them to exit teaching and seek personal equilibrium elsewhere. More generally, within organisations there is a constant potential for conflicts – mostly around small tactical issues – between the newly empowered managers of calculation and enterprise and those whom they strive to call to account. Small acts of resistance and moments of capitulation or compromise tend to contribute to processes of drift and attrition which work to erase principles and change subjectivities piecemeal and without drama. At the same time new entrants come into teaching mostly 'unencumbered' by the older residual subjectivities. There is no simple logic of domination in all of this. The regime of calculation offers opportunities for career progression, for a sense of achievement and triumph, to be happy and tired, and for monetary reward. Foucault

(1983: 232) asserts that: 'My point is not that everything is bad, but that everything is dangerous.' Furthermore, there are, for some, fragile spaces that can be defended and occasionally opportunities arise to reassert old 'truths' and counter-memories.

If there are things that are worth defending within the previous regime of public service, and clearly not everything is, then one component of such a defence must be a proper understanding of the relations of power within which we now find ourselves enmeshed and which shape our present. Such an understanding involves coming to grips with the way in which the mundane techniques and tactics of attrition and change are joined up in an 'ascending' configuration of power and in an identity of relation between the elements. But it is also necessary to appreciate the inconsistencies and ambiguities within the social fields and discourses which enact this identity in practice. And while we need to understand how these elements and their relations enter into us and encourage us to work on ourselves in a variety of ways, we also need to hold firmly onto a sense that we are none of the things we now do, think or desire.[3]

This is a critical precursor to thinking otherwise.

References

Ball, S. J. (2007a) *Education Plc: Understanding private sector participation in public sector education*. London: Routledge.

Ball, S. J. (2007b) 'Privatising education, privatising education policy, privatising educational research: network governance and the "competition state"'. The Routledge Lecture, given at the British Educational Research Association Annual Conference, London.

Barker, I. (2007) 'Academies ask teachers to halve paid maternity leave'. *Times Education Supplement*, 7 December. Online <www.tes.co.uk/search/story/?story_id=2483217> (accessed 6 May 2008).

Baumann, Z. (1991) *Modernity and Ambivalence*. Oxford: Polity Press.

Bernstein, B. (1996) *Pedagogy Symbolic Control and Identity*. London: Taylor and Francis.

Broadhead, L.-A. and Howard, S. (1998) 'The art of punishing: the Research Assessment Exercise and the ritualisation of power in higher education'. *Education Policy Analysis Archives*, 6. Online <http://epaa.asu.edu/epaa/v6n8.html> (accessed 6 May 2008).

Butler, J. (2004) *Undoing Gender*. New York and London: Routledge.

Campbell, C., Evans, J., Askew, S., Hughes, M. and McCallum, B. (2004) *Evaluation of Education Partnership Boards*. London: Institute of Education.

Canaan, J. (2008, forthcoming) 'A funny thing happened on the way to the (European Social) forum: or how new forms of accountability are transforming academics' identities and possible responses'. In W. Shumar and J. Canaan (eds) *Structure and Agency in the Neo-liberal University*. New York: Routledge.

Dalyell, T. (1997) 'Thistle diary: contract culture and net connections – more comment from Westminster'. New Scientist, 18 January, p. 44. Online <http://www.newscientist.com/article/mg15320656.300-thistle-diary--contract-culture-and-net-connections--more-comment-from-westminster-by-bitam-dalyellbi.html (accessed 6 May 2008).

Davies, B. and Petersen, E. B. (2005) 'Neo-liberal discourse and the academy: the forestalling of (collective) resistance'. *Learning and Teaching in the Social Sciences*, 2: 77–9.

Dillabough, J.-A. (1999) 'Gender politics and conceptions of the modern teacher: women, identity and professionalism'. *British Journal of Sociology of Education*, 20: 373–94.

Falk, C. (1999) 'Sentencing learners to life'. *Theory, Technology and Culture*, 22: 19–27.

Foucault, M. (1979) *Discipline and Punish*. Harmondsworth: Penguin.

Foucault, M. (1983) Afterword to *The Subject and Power*. In H. Dreyfus and P. Rabinow (eds) *Michel Foucault: Beyond structuralism and hermeneutics*. Chicago, IL: University of Chicago Press.

Gee, J. (1999) 'New people in new worlds: networks, the new capitalism and schools'. In B. Cope and M. Kalantzis (eds), *Multiliteracies: Literacy learning and the design of social futures*. London: Routledge.

Gray, A. (1997) 'Contract culture and target fetishism: the distortive effects of output measures on local regeneration programmes'. *Local Economy*, 11: 243–57.

Health Sociology Review (2005) *Workplace Health: The injuries of neoliberalism*. Special Issue edited by T. Schofield. *Health Sociology Review*, 14 (1).

Hunter, I. (1996) 'Assembling the school'. In A. Barry, T. Osborne and N. Rose (eds), *Foucault and Political Reason: Liberalism, neo-liberalism and rationalities of government*. London: UCL Press.

Jessop, B. (1998) 'The rise of governance and the risks of failure'. *International Social Science Journal*, 155.

Jessop, B. (2006) 'Globalization and the national state'. In S. Aronowitz and P. Bratsis (eds), *Paradigm Lost: State theory reconsidered*. Minneapolis, MN: University of Minnesota Press.

Kickert, W.J.M., Klijn, E.H. and Koppenjan, J.F.M. (1997) 'Managing networks in the public sector: Findings and reflections'. In Kickert, Klijn and Koppenjan (eds), *Managing Complex Networks: Strategies for the Public Sector*. Thousand Oaks, CA: Sage.

Latour, B. (1987) *Science in Action: How to follow scientists and engineers through society*. Cambridge, MA: Harvard University Press.

Leys, M. (2001) *Market-Driven Politics*. London: Verso.

Lyotard, J.-F. (1984) *The Postmodern Condition: A Report on Knowledge*. Manchester: Manchester University Press.

MacKenzie, R. and Lucio, M.M. (2005) 'The realities of regulatory change: beyond the fetish of deregulation'. *British Journal of Sociology*, 39: 499–517.

MacKinnon, D. (2000) 'Managerialism, governmentality and the state: a neo-Foucauldian approach to local economic governance'. *Political Geography*, 19: 293–314.

Mahony, P., Hextall, I. and Menter, I. (2004a) 'Threshold assessment and performance management: modernizing or masculinizing teaching in England'. *Gender and Education*, 16: 131–49.

Mahony, P., Menter, I. and Hextall, I. (2004b) 'The emotional impact of performance-related pay on teachers in England'. *British Educational Research Journal*, 30: 435–56.

Marinetto, M. (2003) 'Governing beyond the centre: a critique of the anglo-governance school'. *Political Studies*, 51, 592–608.

Morley, L. (2003) *Quality and Power in Higher Education*. Maidenhead: Open University Press.

Newman, J. (2001) *Modernising Governance: New Labour, Policy and Society*. London: Sage.

O'Flynn, G. and Petersen, E.B. (2007) 'The "good life" and the "rich portfolio": young women, schooling and neo-liberal subjectification'. *British Journal of Sociology of Education*, 28: 459–72.

O'Sullivan, D. (2005) *Cultural Politics and Irish Education since the 1950s: Policy Paradigms and Power*. Dublin: Institute of Public Administration.

Patrinos, H.A. (2005) 'Education contracting: scope for future research'. In *Mobilizing the Private Sector for Public Education*, paper given at seminar co-sponsored by the World Bank, Kennedy School of Government, Harvard University.

Perryman, J. (2006) 'Panoptic performativity and school inspection regimes: disciplinary mechanisms and life under special measures'. *Journal of Education Policy*, 21: 147–61.

Perryman, J. (2007) 'Inspection and emotion'. *Cambridge Journal of Education*, 37: 173–90.

Power, M. (1994) *The Audit Explosion*. London: Demos.

Richards, D. and Smith, M.J. (2002) *Governance and Public Policy in the United Kingdom*. Oxford: Oxford University Press.

Rose, N. (1996) 'Governing "advanced" liberal democracies'. In A. Barry, T. Osborne and N. Rose (eds), *Foucault and Political Reason: Liberalism, Neo-liberalism and Rationalities of Government*. London: UCL Press.

Saltman, K.J. (2000) *Collateral Damage: Corporatizing Public Schools – A Threat to Democracy*. Lanham, MD: Rowan and Littlefield.

Saltman, K.J. (2005) *The Edison Schools: Corporate Schooling and the Assault on Public Education*. New York: Routledge.

Shore, C. and Wright, S. (1999) 'Audit culture and anthropology: neo-liberalism in British higher education'. *The Journal of the Royal Anthropological Institute*, 5: 557–75.

Slater, D. and Tonkiss, F. (2001) *Market Society*. Cambridge: Polity Press.

Sparkes, A.C. (2007) 'Embodiment, academics and the audit culture: a story seeking consideration'. *Qualitative Research*, 7: 521–50.

Strathern, M. (1997) 'Improving ratings: audit in the British university system'. *European Review*, 5: 305–21.

Vincent-Jones, P. (2006) *The New Public Contracting: Regulation, responsiveness, relationality.* Oxford: Oxford University Press.

Walzer, M. (1984) *Spheres of Justice: a Defence of Pluralism and Equality.* Oxford: Martin Robertson.

Wittel, A. (2001) 'Towards a network sociality'. *Theory, Culture and Society*, 18: 51–76.

Yeatman, A. (1996) 'The new contractualism: management reform or a new approach to governance?' In G. Davis and P. Weller (eds), *New Ideas, Better Government*. St Leonards, Australia: Allen and Unwin.

Zambeta, E. (2002) 'Modernisation of educational governance in Greece: from state control to state steering'. *European Educational Research Journal*, 1: 637–55.

Notes

[1] I am very grateful to Trinidad Ball, Jane Perryman and Bryan Cunningham for their comments on earlier drafts of this paper.

[2] I use teacher in the broadest sense here to include all those who teach or research in schools, and further and higher education.

[3] To borrow from and paraphrase Nietzsche.

5   Ethical issues in professional life
Ingrid Lunt

Introduction

Ethical conduct, professional integrity and moral probity have long been held to be central features of the 'professional' and, traditionally, codes of ethics constituted one of the hallmarks and defining characteristics of the professions. With a strong basis in self-regulation, the professions were expected to monitor the conduct of their members, to ensure their probity and ethical integrity and, if necessary, to discipline and thus regulate professional behaviour. According to Freidson, 'part of the purpose of .... codes [of ethics] is without doubt to persuade the public that the formulation of ethical standards justifies trust' (2001: 214). A commitment to traditional notions of ethical conduct and ethical codes continues to the present time to constitute a feature not only of well-established professions but also of newer professions and occupational groups aspiring to 'professional' status.

However, the past 30 years or so have seen major changes in society, which imply growing complexity, uncertainty and unpredictability which in turn undermine previous certainties in relation to professional practice. There are a number of factors that contribute to these changes. Increasingly, it is said, we live in a 'risk society' (Beck, 1992) in which the permanent features of uncertainty and unpredictability undermine what were previously considered professional certainties. The electronic and digital revolution, the global information age, the ubiquitous domination of the Internet and the 'knowledge society' threaten the notion of professional expertise and authority and unique knowledge and infallibility. Major changes to the context of professional work, including reforms to the public sector, to professional regulation and to professional monopolies, and the introduction of managerialism and market competition have affected professional practices. The 1970s oil crisis brought financial and economic realities that have affected an economic prosperity enjoyed over many years; the reality of finite resources, infinite demands and contentious priorities has influenced the provision of services, and posed challenges to professional responsibility. The growth of litigation promotes more defensive practices, while the 'blame and shame' culture can create a complex tension between professional loyalty and a search for the public good. Interdisciplinarity and interprofessional collaboration are encouraged and at times mandated by legislation, yet pose major challenges for traditional mono-professional cultures.

These major changes in the nature and context of professional work, reflecting in part wider political, social and economic cultural changes in society both in the UK and globally, arguably pose considerable challenges for the ways in which ethical issues are understood and managed, and for a relevant notion of 'ethical professionalism'. The changes include altered relationships between 'professional' and 'client' (or, as sometimes formulated, 'provider' and 'purchaser') and the growth of 'consumer' power and client empowerment, and a less deferential and better informed public. They also include changed practices as a result of public-sector reform, including the introduction of managerialism, markets and competition. In addition, recent well-publicised and high-profile cases of misconduct and abuse of professional trust and autonomy, in particular involving the traditional professions of law, medicine and accountancy (Sullivan, 2005), have contributed to a questioning of current forms of professional regulation and the idea that the professions can be trusted to ensure the ethical behaviour of their members. This in turn has led to the possibility of greater state intervention and consequent reduced professional autonomy. In fact, reflecting this changed context there have been major regulatory, legislative and procedural changes which constitute features of the 'audit explosion' described by Power (1997), and change the nature of and basis for professional accountability.

For the 'professions', this changed context is also due to changing notions of 'professionalism', and what it means to be a 'professional', changes to the nature of professional work, to a growing focus on the rights of consumers (or, in European Union terminology, the rights of 'citizens'), and to the growth of the widespread use of the Internet which has altered public access to information and expertise and empowered consumers. For many of the major professions there have been substantial changes to the ways in which professionals are regulated, reflecting moves towards the displacement of the welfare state by the regulatory state, and other forms of enhanced governance and control (Power, 1997). In order to achieve greater transparency and accountability, external controls have been imposed on self-regulatory systems and greater state intervention introduced to the regulatory process. Thus 'Professional autonomy gave way to accountability; informal mechanisms of standard setting became more formal; tacit knowledge ... gave way to measurable information available to all (Royal College of Physicians, 2005: 4).

In this chapter I plan to consider the way in which ethical codes have been used to justify society's trust in members of professional bodies, and to discuss some of the ways that these very codes are challenged by some of the changes referred to above. I wish to explore a more modern and possibly more appropriate notion of 'ethical professionalism' than the one that continues to be implied by formal professional codes of ethics. I will consider the implications of this for the ways in which professionals may ensure their ethical practice and justify the trust of the public and society.

Traditional accounts of professionalism

Despite the inherent lack of clarity of definition of 'professional' (Hoyle and John, 1995), traditional accounts of professionalism emphasise the 'knowledge, service, autonomy model' (e.g. Haug, 1973). Early accounts tended to identify traits or features common to traditional professional groups (e.g. Millerson, 1964; Hickson and Thomas, 1969; Freidson, 1994; Siegrist, 1994); these features included the acquisition of a body of specialist knowledge (and higher education and training), the holding of public status (and autonomy), a commitment to service to the public (and altruism), membership of a professional body with a code of ethics (and self-regulation). This is not the place to discuss the relevance of 'trait' theories of professions. It remains the case that codes of ethics and claims to ethical conduct were and remain an *essential characteristic* of the 'traditional' professions, and of traditional notions of professionalism, and have been perpetuated in moves to 'professionalisation' by newer occupational groups (Lunt and Majors, 2000).

The traditional professions established early on in their existence a professional body which was intended to ensure high standards of education and conduct, regulate entry to the ranks of the profession, maintain a code of professional conduct (or ethical code), and, in some cases, monitor and discipline their own members. According to this traditional model, professionals practised on the basis of their (unique) specialist expertise, exercised judgement, including ethical judgement, and were placed in a position of trust by their clients, by the public and, implicitly, by the state. The relationship between medical doctors and their patients, or lawyers and their clients, for example, tended to be one of client subservience and deference, knowledge and power imbalance, and based on a trust that the professional 'knew best' and would act always in the best interests of the patient or client, drawing on notions of unique expertise, altruism and professional infallibility.

This trust, and the notion of professional infallibility, both in terms of competence and of moral probity, led to an implicit arrangement where professionals had a 'special relationship' with society,

> the essence of which is that professions are given greater autonomy than other social groups. (They) set their own standards, regulate entry into their own ranks, discipline their members, and operate with fewer restraints than the arts, trades or business. In return they are expected to serve the public good and enforce high standards of conduct and discipline.
>
> (Skrtic, 1991: 87)

Professions have been enabled by this 'special relationship' to justify professional monopolies and maintain the protection of their professional title, and freedom from competition that has tended to characterise many professional groups. Thus, according to Rueschmeyer:

> individually and, in association, collectively the professions 'strike a bargain' with society in which they exchange competence and integrity against the trust of clients and community, freedom from lay supervision and interference, protection from unqualified competition as well as substantial remuneration and higher social status. As guarantees of this self-control they point to careful recruitment and training, formal organisation, codes of ethics and professional courts or committees enforcing these codes ...
>
> (1983: 41)

This 'bargain' (or social contract) and the ability of professions to protect their title and thereby to hold a monopoly over an area of work is a major aspect of the professional 'project', justified through claims of public protection. This monopoly has been achieved in large part on the basis of their specialist (unique) expertise and their commitment to an ethical code which, traditionally, protected them from state interference, and enabled them to regulate themselves, through forms of 'self-regulation'.

Self-regulation depends on the existence of ethical codes, which, it is maintained, helps to ensure these high standards of conduct and discipline. Accompanying disciplinary procedures regulate the behaviour of members under the practice of self-regulation, which is organised through the professional body.[1]

Ethical codes and self-regulation

The possession of an ethical code and the means to enforce members' adherence to it continue to constitute a central feature of the way in which the 'professions' practise and are organised. Membership of a professional association or body entails a commitment to abide by the code of ethics and conduct, and infringement may lead to punishment by members of that professional body (the most extreme being expulsion, and, for statutorily regulated professions, the temporary or permanent prohibition from practice of that profession). Thus, for example, medical doctors, regulated by statute, may be 'struck off' the register and debarred from practice following serious misconduct. Indeed, this is a central aspect of claims by the professions to protection of the public.

The claim has served as a major plank of the attempts by a number of professional bodies, for example the British Psychological Society (BPS), the professional body for psychologists, to gain statutory regulation, and thus protection of the title 'psychologist'. At the present time, the BPS maintains a voluntary register of 'Chartered Psychologists' (a form of title protection of the term 'chartered psychologist'), for which it is seeking statutory endorsement. The voluntary nature of the Register of Chartered Psychologists means that is currently possible for anyone to call themselves a 'psychologist', and to work as such, whatever their academic and professional qualifications, and whatever their ethical commitments, or lack thereof. The push for statutory regulation (and claims to protect the public against the unqualified) has been played out mainly in the arena of this professional body (the BPS) which sets standards of academic and professional qualification, which has a well-developed code of ethics and which disciplines its members. According to this body,

> statutory regulation exists to ensure standards of practice by regulated practitioners and to protect the public as far as possible against the risks of poor practice. It works by setting agreed standards of practice and competence, by registering those who are competent to practise and restricting the use of specified titles to those who are registered. It can also apply sanctions such as removing from the register any practitioner whose fitness to practise is impaired ... the [British Psychological] Society has long argued that a statutory system is necessary to protect the public from charlatans and poor practice
>
> (British Psychological Society, 2007: 1)

This body argues that voluntary regulation and voluntary adherence to an ethical code, such as currently exists, is not sufficient to protect the public, and that only statutory regulation will achieve the assurance of a psychologist's 'fitness to practise' and thus public protection.

Ethical codes aim to promote 'ethical behaviour' and 'ethical standards of behaviour'. Although the ethical codes of different professional groups, and indeed different 'Western' countries, tend to embody similar overarching ethical principles such as *respect, competence, responsibility* and *integrity*, they tend to be aspirational rather than prescriptive. It would be hard to disagree with these ethical principles, yet their very abstract nature tends to give them a distance from the professional practice that they are intended to regulate.

According to Freidson, codes of ethics perform a 'translation function, dealing with the use of specialised skills in circumstances not familiar to lay people but involving familiar sins' (2001: 215). Yet it is generally agreed that ethical codes serve a dual function, on the one hand being aspirational and guiding professionals towards optimal conduct, while on the other hand being used for a regulatory function in defining standards that clients can expect and countering malpractice. The revised code of the BPS claims that the 'code has been written primarily to guide not to punish' (British Psychological Society, 2006: 6). Very few ethical codes prescribe behaviour and provide guidance on the 'do's and don'ts' of ethical behaviour. In this way they are very different from a code such as the Highway Code which provides clear and prescriptive guidance as to how to drive a vehicle and behave on the public highway.

The recently revised *Code of Ethics and Conduct* of the BPS (British Psychological Society, 2006) acknowledges that 'psychologists are likely to need to make decisions in difficult, changing and unclear situations' and that 'no Code can replace the need for psychologists to use their professional and ethical judgement'. Thus it claims:

The British Psychological Society recognises its obligation to set and uphold the highest standards of professionalism, and to promote ethical behaviour, attitudes and judgements on the part of psychologists by:

- being mindful of the need for protection of the public

- expressing clear ethical principles, values and standards

- promoting such standards by education and consultation

- developing and implementing methods to help psychologists monitor their professional behaviour and attitudes

- investigating complaints of unethical behaviour, taking corrective action when appropriate, and learning from experience

- assisting psychologists with ethical decision making

- providing opportunities for discourse on these issues.

(British Psychological Society, 2006)

The code is based on the four ethical principles of *respect, competence, responsibility* and *integrity*, which are then described in Statements of Values and further defined by a set of standards 'setting out the ethical conduct that the Society expects of its members' (British Psychological Society, 2006: 6).

A different approach has been taken by the General Teaching Council (GTC) in its short *Statement of Professional Values and Practice for Teachers* (General Teaching Council, 2006a: 1) which 'sets out the beliefs, values and attitudes that make up teacher professionalism', and is separate from the *Code of Conduct and Practice for Registered Teachers* which sets out 'minimum standards for the regulation of the profession' beginning with a section on 'unacceptable professional conduct' (General Teaching Council, 2006b). Similarly, the General Medical Council (GMC), the body that regulates the practice of medical doctors, has recently developed its *Good Medical Practice* (General Medical Council, 2006) which 'sets out the principles and values on which good practice is founded' and which forms the basis for the GMC regulatory function. The GMC makes explicit:

> We have strong and effective legal powers designed to maintain the standards the public have a right to expect of doctors. We are not here to protect the medical profession – their interests are protected by others. Our job is to protect patients ... this concept of 'professionally-led regulation in partnership with the public' enables the GMC to set a framework of standards and ethics that is owned by the profession while reflecting the views and expectations of the public
>
> (General Medical Council, 2008)

However, formal professional ethical codes are only one source of the values, attitudes and beliefs that inform an individual professional's behaviour and that contribute to their understanding of moral and ethical behaviour. Professional values are informed by a wide range of different influences, arguably more complex and potentially conflicting, in a context of greater unpredictability, fewer certainties, and a growing globalisation.

Professional values

Individual professional values are informed by a range of different influences, which include the family, the peer group, religious beliefs, cultural and community norms, political convictions, ideological commitments, social or community norms and values, agency or employer policy, individual conscience, and personal values. In a study exploring professional competencies, Eraut and colleagues identified four sets of values that impinged on ethical conduct at work: legal values, values of the profession, values of individual professionals, and values of employing organisations (Eraut, 1994). In many cases, these values and beliefs which contribute to an individual's morality and sense of self may be as strong as or stronger than the values transmitted by a professional code.

The diverse origins of professionals' attitudes, beliefs and values result in a complex and multifaceted situation where an individual professional may experience conflicts and tensions between personal and professional values, and between personal beliefs and professional duties. In some cases, this may lead to profound ethical dilemmas which cannot be resolved by recourse to formal ethical codes and require more fundamental and nuanced consideration. Even though there is widespread agreement both internationally and across different professional groups as to fundamental ethical principles that guide 'ethical' behaviour (Gauthier, 2005), their very formality and abstract nature may not help the individual professional faced with a complex ethical dilemma in a situation of professional isolation. Nash (1996) has argued that professionals in general rarely if ever consult such codes when considering ethical dilemmas. Given the potential fallibility of ethical codes to regulate behaviour, can the 'special relationship' between professionals and society continue to be justified?

The 'special relationship' under threat?

Trust in the efficacy of self-regulation through the power of ethical codes and their disciplinary procedures has been one of the central facets of the 'special relationship' that the professions have forged with society and with the state. This special relationship began to come under attack with the neo-liberal reforms of the 1980s, and in particular the claim that professions are self-interest groups, self-serving and protecting their members rather than the public. For example:

> given the poor track record of systems based on professional codes of ethics and self-disciplinary action as a means of protecting the public, what reason do we have to be confident that (statutory regulation) will not largely function as window-dressing disguising the professional self-interest as has so often been the case?
>
> (Mowbray, 1995: 84)

Nevertheless, professionals have continued to hold the power, status and influence that have historically been part of the 'professional project' and, according to Armstrong (1995:121), 'despite the challenge to professional autonomy that is implicit in the neo-liberal reforms of the 1980s and 1990s, professionals continue to pursue their interests within the administrative bureaucracy of the state'.

The past ten years have seen a major shift in this 'administrative bureaucracy'. Although occupational groups employed within the public sector have been contrasted with so-called 'liberal' professionals and considered 'semi-professionals' (Etzioni, 1969), with their more restricted knowledge, autonomy and responsibility (and status), both groups have been affected by the gradual privatisation of welfare and by the systematic undermining of professional monopolies. This has been accompanied by the changed relationships between service providers and service users (the purchaser/provider relationship) both in terms of individual clients, and in terms of the wider commissioning of services by agencies such as local authorities and other commissioning agencies. Thus services may increasingly be offered by a range of providers leading to a very different relationship and a very different understanding of trust.

Questions concerning the nature of the trust placed in professionals have been raised in reaction to a small number of well-publicised instances by professionals of abuse of trust. Examples from the field of medicine have attracted strong media interest and led to major changes in legislation. The Bristol Royal Infirmary Inquiry into the deaths of 29 babies undergoing heart surgery in the late 1980s and early 1990s 'lifted the lid on an "old boys'" culture among doctors; patients being left in the dark about treatment ... secrecy about doctors' performance, and a lack of external monitoring of NHS performance' (Butler, 2002: 10). The report of the Inquiry, published in 2001, led to a number of new measures, including new health legislation and the introduction of bodies to monitor the performance of healthcare professionals. This report coincided with another widely publicised report, that of the Alder Hey Inquiry into the unauthorised, unethical and illegal retention of human organs, and the report of the Shipman Inquiry which found the English medical practitioner guilty of the murders of 215 patients, and 45 other suspicious deaths. Although these were extreme examples involving maverick individuals, the media were quick to condemn and to ask: how could this be allowed to happen? Can the professions be trusted?

Are we facing a crisis of trust?

In her 2002 Reith Lectures for the BBC, Onora O'Neill posed the following questions:

> Are we facing a crisis of trust? ... what does it take for us to place trust in others? What evidence do we need to place it well? Are human rights and democracy the basis for a society in which trust can be placed, or does trust need other conditions? Does the revolution in accountability support or undermine trust?
>
> (O'Neill, 2002: 5)

From examples such as those mentioned above, and the ensuing public outcry, it would appear that professionals may be facing a crisis of trust. Even though it concerns a tiny minority of individuals, the behaviour of once trusted professionals such as those described above has enabled the media to arouse in the public what O'Neill terms a 'culture of suspicion'. Part of this culture and the diminution of public trust (whether justified or not) has led to the 'audit explosion' and new concepts of accountability:

> the new accountability culture aims at ever more perfect administrative control of institutional and professional life ... the new legislation, regulation and controls ... require detailed conformity to procedures and protocols, detailed record-keeping and provision of information in specified formats and success in reaching targets.
>
> (O'Neill, 2002: 46)

Instead of 'trust' in professional judgement, the introduction of 'performance measurement', targets, outcomes-based evaluation, and bureaucratic form-filling in every professional arena has shifted the basis of professional work, trust and accountability. Indeed, a major assault on professionals in the United Kingdom has been fuelled in part by the Government and in part by the media, with the Government responding by ever tighter regulation and control, while the media have fanned public anxiety, moral panic and outrage by sensationalising maverick individuals such as Harold Shipman.

Yet, as O'Neill suggests, professionals continue to be trusted albeit with caveats (for example the search for 'second', or even third, 'opinions') and in general we continue to operate on the basis of a relationship of trust when we require professional expertise.

A new form of professional regulation?

A number of governmental and consumer initiatives emerged in the wake of anxieties about the ability of professions to regulate the behaviour of their own members. In 1997 the Government appointed its Better Regulation Task Force to provide advice on how to improve the quality of its regulation, and how to control major professions of greatest risk such as medicine, accounting or legal services. These had had a significant degree of self-regulation in which, at the time, professions regulated themselves and members of the same profession would act as defendant and judge.

In contrast to other European countries where the state has a much stronger and more direct role in professional regulation, the UK has tended to rely on professional self-regulation. The Better Regulation Task Force and the newly formed Better Regulation Commission have attempted to find the most effective point on the continuum of degrees of regulation (from state regulation to self-regulation) while achieving greater accountability, consistency and transparency. This has led to strengthening the power of 'lay' members (i.e. individuals from outside the professional group) on all regulatory councils, and an increasing separation of the regulatory authority from the professional body, in efforts to distance the regulation of the profession from the activities of the profession itself. These developments have signalled a new form of professional accountability and government control. Writing abut the profession of medicine, Ham suggests:

> Not least, these initiatives sent out a clear signal that self-regulation was no longer seen as sufficient to safeguard standards and patients. The adoption of these policies was possible because of the accumulation of evidence that existing arrangements for ensuring quality were inadequate.
>
> (Ham, 1999: 169)

At about the same time, the Consumers Association (CA) report *Leave it to the Professionals* questioned the ability of professions to regulate themselves and suggested that 'it can be difficult for the public to believe that self-regulation is not synonymous with self-interest' (Consumers Association, 1998: i). Reflecting the shift in discourse (to the more modern concept 'service providers') the CA asks:

> what is it about one particular set of service providers that means that we tend to trust them more than others? Crucially is this trust well placed and if it isn't, are there sufficient measures in place to ensure that we are adequately protected if things go wrong?
>
> (Consumers Association, 1998:1)

It is clear that the 'protection' of traditional ethical codes administered by traditional professional bodies may not be sufficient to allay the anxieties of a public that has been persuaded by the media that professionals are not to be trusted. There is also evidence from professionals themselves that ethical codes in themselves are not sufficient to ensure ethical behaviour (Guiney, 2007).

A modern ethical professionalism

> Given the changed context for professional work, the epistemological, social, cultural and regulatory challenges discussed above, and the wider challenges resulting from increased internationalisation, multiculturalism and globalisation, what might be the features of a more modern ethical professionalism, or how are professionals to assure the ethical behaviour which justifies public trust in the current situation? How can we be sure that professionals merit 'the trust they proclaim themselves worthy of receiving'?
>
> (Koehn, 1994: 11)

Traditional ethical codes have tended to be based on a somewhat positivistic and rule-bound framework which informs a prescriptive and disciplinary approach to professional behaviour. Koehn describes this as a 'male' ethic where 'ethical reasoning qualifies as mature only if it decides ethical dilemmas by employing universal principles and appealing to a hierarchy of rights' (1998: 2). She further points out that traditional ethics have tended to employ Western scientific methodologies, ignoring the contribution of other ways of seeing the world, for example feminist or those derived from other cultures and philosophies. It is therefore important that professionals develop 'ethical literacy' (Webster and Lunt, 2002) and ethical sensitivity, and the ability to 'read' the ethical complexities of the individual professional situation, in order to ensure that practice is characterised by 'wise judgement under conditions of considerable uncertainty' (Eraut, 1994).

In his discussion of the role of the professional of the third millennium, Bottery (1998) proposes five ethics that should inform the professional practice of the future: an ethic of *provisionality*, an ethic of *truth searching*, an ethic of *reflective integrity*, an ethic of *humility*, and an ethic of *humanistic education*. These are very different ethical principles from those evidenced in traditional codes of ethics, and reflect some of the values of feminism, other cultures, and the uncertainty, unpredictability and contestability both of professional contexts and of professional knowledge.

An ethic of *provisionality* accepts the contested and provisional nature of knowledge, and the existence and validity of diverse viewpoints and beliefs. It implies a greater degree of negotiation and acknowledgement of mutual expertise rather than the traditional hierarchical model of expertise and authority, and the paternalism of assumptions of professional infallibility. The recognition that truth is not absolute implies a greater tolerance and acceptance of uncertainty and 'provisionality'. An ethic of *truth searching*, means being prepared to struggle to understand complexity and, if necessary, to tolerate ambivalence and discomfort. It also involves a degree of courage in the contemplation of potentially uncomfortable truths. The ethic of *reflective integrity* acknowledges the complexity of each situation and the value-laden and culture-bound nature of many professional judgements. In this way it echoes the stance put forward by Schön (1983, 1987), and the need for professional practice to transcend 'technical rationality' and to develop reflexivity. Professionals need, above all, to show an ethic of *humility* and accept that 'personal fallibility is not a failing but a condition of being human' (Bottery, 1998) and that it is possible for professionals to make mistakes; in this context it is essential to admit and to learn from mistakes. Finally, an ethic of *humanistic education* such as that espoused by Carl Rogers (1983) involves dialogue and empowerment, and Rogers' three fundamental conditions of genuineness, unconditional positive regard and empathic understanding.

These forms of ethic are rooted in epistemological and paradigmatic frameworks which are very different from the positivistic and rational paradigm implicit in formal codes of ethics, and they call into question the traditional notion of expertise, and the power implied by that expertise. We live in an altogether more fragile professional world, where professionals and clients alike are struggling to understand the pressures, tensions and dilemmas that constitute the context in which we find ourselves.

In this professional world it is possible to extend and amplify the traditional ethical principles of competence, respect, integrity and responsibility, and include the important principle of caring for others (Noddings, 1993). It is further possible to integrate Bottery's five 'radical' principles with traditional ethical principles to reflect the condition described by Barnett:

> In an age of fast globalization, frames of understanding are rent asunder. It is an age of fragility characterized by contestability, challengeability, unpredictability, and uncertainty. This fragility has impact on individuals and institutions and invokes both epistemologies (how we know the world) and ontologies (how we live in such a world)
>
> (Barnett, 2001: 29)

Extending the ethical principles

Competence

A reframed understanding of competence accepts the provisional, contested and changing nature of knowledge, and therefore competence. Traditional notions of professional competence conferred a lifelong licence to practise on those who achieved the entry qualification, and who met the standards set by the professional body. It is now accepted that this is far from adequate and that professionals need to learn from experience and to update their competence and ensure that their knowledge, skills and understanding are up to date. This acceptance underlies the widespread moves to lifelong learning, continuous professional development (CPD) and revalidation as a formal and compulsory part of the licence to practise which have emerged as part of the professions' commitment to enhanced professional practice (Lunt, 2002).

An extended notion of competence implies the ability and willingness to learn from mistakes, to reflect on practice (and see Schön, 1987) and to think through situations that were successful and those that were less so. This realisation has been reflected in the forms of evidence required by a number of professions as part of the revalidation process; a number of professions require the development of a portfolio of practice where the individual professional reflects on their practice, records mistakes or uncomfortable professional encounters, and develops the kind of reflexivity that is part of skilled professional competence. This requires a degree of humility that permits the acknowledgement of error and engenders the motivation to learn and have the courage to deal differently with the next situation. Transcending traditional definitions of competence, this takes us into the field of lifelong learning and continuous improvement, and the acceptance that qualification at a certain time is time-limited and not a qualification for life.

Respect

Reframing and extending the notion of respect implies professionals developing the ability to listen and to empower clients to solve problems themselves when this is appropriate and possible. It involves an attempt to achieve greater equity and mutual understanding, and to accept that clients frequently know 'what is best' and that their views should be accorded validity along the lines of 'complementary expertise'. Demands for a partnership approach to the provision of services require a new form of mutual respect between professional and client and between different professional groups. Inter-professional collaboration and teamwork demand a different mode of relating to other professionals, and an extended notion of respect and acceptance. A reframed notion of respect also implies humility, a principle that is found in Chinese codes of ethics though not in Western codes.

An extended understanding of the principle of respect entails a respect for the inherent dignity of all human beings, an acceptance of the value and power of diverse views and values, regardless of gender, culture, social or other background, and a stance of empathy, caring and compassion. Koehn (1998: 53) puts forward the 'practice of empathy understood as the practice of trying to meet other people on their own terms'. She quotes Meyers (1987) who contends that 'empathy is necessary if we are truly to respect difference among people' (Koehn, 1998: 54). This stance requires the professional to 'stand outside' the traditional professional–client relationship and to acknowledge the uniqueness of the individual and the potential vulnerability inherent in the professional relationship, and to engage in 'empathic' deliberation, and caring.

Integrity

Professional integrity, or 'wholeness' implies, above all, self-awareness and the realisation of our own values, prejudices, beliefs, limitations and fallibility. An extended understanding of professional integrity involves the development of reflexivity, and the ability to reflect on the professional relationship, the effect that this relationship has on both parties, and a commitment to ethical 'intelligence' and 'sensitivity' in relation to the professional task. This embraces Bottery's ethic of reflective integrity through which 'the professional presents an example of a role model to the client which illustrates not simply the nature of professional practice, but more importantly the multi-layered value-laden nature of such practice, and of the society within which it takes place' (Bottery, 1998: 168). This also implies that claims to professional infallibility may be outmoded and that a more cautious approach of iterative and reflexive exploration may be more appropriate.

Responsibility

An extended understanding of professional responsibility involves an acceptance of the dilemmas inherent in professional work. The increasing complexity of the professional–client relationship calls into question the lines of professional responsibility and therefore accountability. The simple one-to-one relationship between professional and client implied in traditional accounts of professionalism has given way to other forms of relationship, sometimes mediated by other agencies. This has led to a number of different dilemmas and challenges. First, there are economic dilemmas. With finite resources, infinite demands and contentious priorities, professionals are required to take bold decisions, whether in the field of medicine, education or social care. These dilemmas are particularly acute within public-sector provision and provide challenges to the notion of the welfare state, and potential tensions to professionals and their values. Second, there are epistemological dilemmas reflecting the contestability and provisionality of knowledge. Yet professionals have a responsibility to work towards a professional ethic that promotes evidence-based practice with demonstrable value to clients (and, increasingly, value for money for agencies and employers). Finally, there are dilemmas inherent in conceptions of professional loyalty and culture. Professionals have a duty to 'speak out' and to make comment on issues of importance (Barnett, 1997). Thus Downie (1990) refers to:

> the duty to speak out with authority on matters of social justice and social utility ... doctors have a duty to speak out on broad issues of health, as for example they may speak out against cigarette advertising or cast doubt on the feasibility of medical services
>
> (Downie, 1990:153)

Yet another area where professionals have a responsibility to speak out involves 'whistle-blowing'. In order to allay accusations of being self-serving and protecting their own, professionals have a responsibility to speak out against members of their own 'clan' (profession) where there is evidence of concern. This responsibility challenges deeply held notions of professional loyalty and culture.

Implications for future professional practice

Ethical codes and a commitment to their use to ensure ethical practice and to discipline professionals continue to constitute a central feature of the 'professional project'. However, widespread changes in society that affect the nature and context of professional work, the relationships between the professions and their clients and the professions and the state, and the role of the professions in society mean that we need to embrace a more modern ethical professionalism. Ethical codes have been used as the basis of the trust accorded to professionals by the public and the state; this trust must be shown to be earned and deserved. There are various ways in which a more modern ethical professionalism should be pursued. Professional bodies themselves have increasingly embraced the practice of CPD and revalidation, frequently linked to licence to practise. Individual professionals are encouraged to work in teams, to discuss their practice and to engage in joint problem-solving. The process of revision of ethical codes has provided an opportunity for professional bodies to articulate the complexity of ethical decision-making and encourage reflective practice, peer support, and other ways to support the development of ethical intelligence. Above all, it is essential that professionals are educated and trained in this important area in order that they develop the relevant knowledge and understanding, and the necessary disposition for self-evaluation and learning from colleagues and experience. Ethical knowledge is not static and factual, but rather dynamic, context dependent and requires a dialogic approach to problem-solving. As professional practitioners are increasingly becoming researching professionals, this provides the opportunity not only for rigorous reflection on practice, but also for engagement with the development of university research ethical procedures and the assurance of ethical research practice. This provides a link between research and practice, and also enables professional practice to be informed by an ethic of research reflexivity, and professional research to be informed by an ethic of practice integrity.

References

Armstrong, D. (1995) *Power and Partnership in Education*. London: Routledge.

Barnett, R. (1997) *Higher Education: a Critical Business*. Buckingham: Open University Press and SRHE.

Barnett, R. (2001) 'Managing universities in a Supercomplex age'. In M. Cutright (ed.) *Chaos Theory and Higher Education. Leadership, Planning and Policy*. New York: Peter Lang.

Beck, U. (1992) *Risk Society. Towards a New Modernity*. London: Sage.

Bottery, M. (1998) *Professionals and Policy: Management Strategy in a Competitive World*. London: Cassell.

British Psychological Society (2006) *Code of Ethics and Conduct*. Leicester: British Psychological Society.

British Psychological Society (2007) *Statutory Regulation – Your Questions Answered*. Leicester: British Psychological Society.

Butler, P. (2002) 'The Bristol Royal Infirmary inquiry: the issue explained'. *Guardian*, 17 January: 10.

Consumers Association (1998) *Leave it to the Professionals*. London: Consumers Association.

Downie, R.S. (1990) 'Professions and professionalism'. *Journal of Philosophy of Education*, 24 (2): 147–59.

Eraut, M. (1994) *Developing Professional Knowledge and Competence*. London: Falmer Press.

Etzioni, A. (ed.) (1969) *The Semi Professions and their Organisations: Teachers, Nurses, Social Workers*. London: Collier McMillan.

Freidson, E. (1994) *Professionalism Reborn. Theory, Prophecy, and Policy*. Cambridge: Polity Press.

Freidson, E. (2001) *Professionalism. The Third Logic*. Cambridge: Polity Press.

Gauthier, J. (2005) 'Towards a universal declaration of ethical principles for psychologists'. In M.J. Stevens and D. Wedding (eds), *Psychology: IUPsyS Global Resource*. Hove: Psychology Press.

General Medical Council (2006) *Good Medical Practice*. London: GMC.

General Medical Council (2008) *GMC HomePage*. Online. <www.gmc-uk.org/about/role/index.asp> (accessed 4 January 2008).

General Teaching Council (2006a) *The Statement of Professional Values and Practice for Teachers*. London: GTC.

General Teaching Council (2006b) *Code of Conduct and Practice for Registered Teachers. Setting Minimum Standards for the Regulation of the Profession*. London: GTC.

Guiney, D. (2007) 'Educational psychologists' accounts of ethically troubling incidents at a time of rapid change in their workplace.' Draft of DEdPsy thesis, Institute of Education, University of London.

Ham, C. (1999) *Health Policy in Britain. The Politics and Organisation of the National Health Service*. London: Macmillan Press.

Haug, M. R. (1973) 'Deprofessionalisation: an alternate hypothesis for the future'. *Sociological Review Monographs*, 20: 195–211.

Hickson, D.J. and Thomas M.W. (1969) 'Professionalization in Britain: a preliminary measurement'. *Sociology*, 3: 37–53.

Hoyle, E. and John, P.D. (1995) *Professional Knowledge and Professional Practice*. London: Cassell.

Koehn, D. (1994) *The Ground of Professional Ethics*. London: Routledge.

Koehn, D. (1998) *Rethinking Feminist Ethics. Care, Trust and Empathy*. London: Routledge.

Lunt, I. (2002) 'Competence, fitness to practise and continuing professional development: the ethical basis of educational psychologists' practice'. *Educational and Child Psychology*, 19 (1): 70–80.

Lunt, I. and Majors K. (2000) 'The professionalisation of educational psychology. Challenges to practice'. *Educational Psychology in Practice*, 15 (4): 237–45.

Meyers, D.T. (1987) 'The socialized individual and individual autonomy: an intersection between philosophy and psychology'. In E.F. Kittay and D.T. Meyers (eds), *Women and Moral Theory*. Totowa, NJ: Rowman and Littlefield.

Millerson, G. (1964) *The Qualifying Associations: a Study in Professionalisation*. London: Routledge.

Mowbray, R. (1995) *The Case Against Psychotherapy Registration*. London: Trans Marginal Press.

Nash, R.J. (1996) *Real World Ethics: Frameworks for Educators and Human Service Professionals*. New York: Teachers College Press.

Noddings, N. (1993) 'Caring: a feminist perspective'. In K.A. Strike and P.L. Ternasky (eds), *Ethics for Professionals in Education: Perspectives for Preparation and Practice*. New York: Teachers College Press.

O'Neill, O. (2002) *A Question of Trust. The BBC Reith Lectures 2002*. Cambridge: Cambridge University Press.

Power, M. (1997) *The Audit Society*. Oxford: Oxford University Press.

Rogers, C. (1983) *Freedom to Learn for the 80s*. Columbus OH: Charles E. Merrill.

Royal College of Physicians (2005) *Doctors in Society. Medical Professionalism in a Changing World. Report of a Working Party*. London: Royal College of Physicians.

Rueschemeyer, D. (1983) 'Professional autonomy and the social control of expertise'. In R. Dingwall and P. Lewis (eds), *The Sociology of the Professions*. London: Macmillan.

Schön, D. (1983) *The Reflective Practitioner: How Professionals Think in Action*. New York: Basic Books.

Schön, D. (1987) *Educating the Reflective Practitioner*. San Francisco CA: Jossey Bass.

Siegrist, H. (1994) 'The professions, State and Government in theory and history'. In T. Bulcher (ed.), *Government and Professional Education*. Buckingham: OUP.

Skrtic, T.M. (1991) *Behind Special Education: a Critical Analysis of Professional Culture and School Organization*. Denver CO: Love Publishing Co.

Sullivan, W.M. (2005) *Work and Integrity: the Crisis and Promise of Professionalism in America*. New York: Jossey-Bass.

Webster, A. and Lunt, I. (2002) 'Ethics, professionalism and the future landscape of educational psychology'. *Educational and Child Psychology*, 19 (1): 97–107.

Note

[1] Many countries outside the UK effect disciplinary regulation by other means, many involving the state itself.

6 The micropolitics of professionalism: power and collective identities in higher education
Louise Morley

Theorising micropolitics

Power is a central constituent of professional relations. It can be overt in the form of decision-making, resource allocation, accreditation and assessment. Power is also present in everyday transactions that can frequently confound and confuse and leave actors unsure of their readings of complex interpersonal encounters. The conceptual framework of micropolitics is an analytical corrective to the many untheorised self-help manuals and the disembodied and socially decontextualised texts on organisational change. Whereas exploration of the concept of professionalism tends to incorporate the core tenets of skills, authority of knowledge, autonomy and standards (Middlehurst, 2000), micropolitics focuses on the ways in which power underpins these areas and is relayed in quotidian practices. It discloses the subterranean conflicts, competitions and minutiae of social relations and describes how power is relayed through seemingly trivial incidents and transactions. In this chapter, I shall attempt to summarise some of the key theorisations of micropolitics. I will also discuss research findings on micropolitical practices from my studies in three continents that have been exploring how equity interventions in higher education institutions (HEIs) are promoted or impeded.

Micropolitical theory started to emerge in the 1960s as an analytical tool for theorising the complexities of organisational change (Burns, 1961; Iannaccone, 1975). It was elaborated conceptually, empirically and ethnographically, by key theorists in the 1980s and 1990s including Ball (1987), Hoyle (1982, 1999), Blase (1991) and Marshall and Scribner (1991). Poststructuralism and postmodernism were prominent theoretical dispositions at that time and micropolitical theory articulated with Foucault's (1979) concept of capillary power to help illuminate how power is transacted in the quotidian. This new conceptual grammar helped to construct and represent organisations as political arenas. The framework of micropolitics revealed the increasingly subtle and sophisticated ways in which dominance is achieved in organisations. Blase (1991: 1) defined micropolitics as being:

> about power and how people use it to influence others and to protect themselves. It is about conflict and how people compete with each other to get what they want. It is about co-operation and how people build support among themselves to achieve their ends.

Hoyle (1999) suggested that micropolitics can be divided into policy and management. The former relates to how staff respond to external pressures, e.g. resistance, retreatism, ritualism. Whereas management micropolitics concerns the strategies whereby leaders and professionals pursue their interests in the context of the management of the organisation. He argued that different 'mixes' of interests: individual, professional, managerial, policy-oriented, political, etc. are important ingredients in micropolitics. Indeed, it can also be argued that micropolitics is an essential component of management, particularly the management of change.

Bacharach and Mundell (1993) suggested that Weber's 'logic of action' is the preferred approach, that interest groups (coalitions) rather than the individual or the organisation is the preferred unit of analysis and that the political analysis of organisations should interrelate micro- and macropolitical approaches. Ball's influential work combined the individual with the organisation and interest representation. It contributed to the naming of the shadow or subtext in professional and organisational life by suggesting that there is a way of conceptualising a 'darker side' of organisational life (Ball, 1987: 270). By naming power as a major driver and energy source in professional life, the bland constructs of organisational science were revisioned.

Table 6.1: Ball's key concepts

Micropolitical perspective	Organisational science
Power	Authority
Goal diversity	Goal coherence
Ideological disputation	Ideological neutrality
Conflict	Consensus
Interests	Motivation
Political activity	Decision-making
Control	Consent

Source: Ball, 1987: 8

The idea that beneath or beyond the surface rationality was a mass of conflicts, tensions, resentments, competing interests and power imbalances that influence everyday transactions in organisations captured the imaginations of change agents struggling to understand why logical and rational interventions for change, such as anti-discriminatory legislation, were floundering in their application (Morley, 1999).

The invisible and intangible nature of power has been a preoccupation of theorists of micropolitics. Underpinning much of the understanding of micropolitics is the elusive sense that something is going on which cannot be satisfactorily named or described. Blase and Anderson (1995: 13) suggested that in a postmodern world, power is used and structured into social relations so that it does not appear to be 'used' at all. Hence there was a subtle shift from the material to the abstract or symbolic. The concept of symbolic violence – particularly in relation to male dominance – was applied to organisational and professional life in the 1990s (Hearn, 1994). Ball (1994: 27) reminded us that, according to Foucault:

> the real political task is to criticise the working of institutions which appear to be both neutral and independent, and to criticise them in such a manner that the political violence which has always exercised itself obscurely through them will be unmasked so that we can fight them.

The quixotic quality of much micropolitical activity can be because it tends to involve relationships rather than structures, informal knowledge rather than formal information, identities rather than roles, skills rather than designated organisational positions and, most importantly, talk rather than paper. One example is the formal written reference for an applicant's promotion or recruitment that could be regulated by data protection legislation, accompanied by an informal phone call or casual discussion in which comments are less guarded. Counter-hegemonic scholars have sometimes used micropolitical theory to attempt to understand how rational interventions for change, e.g. equality policies, appear to have achieved such minimal impact in both qualitative and quantitative terms (Deem *et al.*, 2005).

Gender analysis of organisations has also utilised micropolitical constructs. Troubled and mystified as to why gender discrimination and social inequalities continued to exist despite decades of anti-discriminatory legislation, feminist scholars have looked to micropolitical theory to analyse gender, identity and social and professional groups (Paechter, 1995; Reay, 1998; Morley, 1999; Budgeon, 2001; Benjamin, 2002). Feminist theorists (e.g. Butler, 1999) have long argued that gender is not a given, but is in continual production. It is reproduced in positionings, judgements and relations that occur on a daily and personal basis. In other words, gender is a verb as well as a noun, and we constantly 'do' gender.

In the beginning of the twenty-first century, micropolitical theory is also being applied to the analysis of how neo-liberal policy reforms and interventions for change have been incorporated, resisted or performed by different professional groups. The audit culture, its impact on professional identities, and the insertion of quality assurance discourses and practices into employment regimes have elicited several studies (Milliken, 2001; Morley, 2003, 2005; Kelchtermans, 2007). Leadership, teacher development and school effectiveness have also been analysed micropolitically (Altrichter and Salzgeber, 2000; Kelchtermans and Ballet, 2002 and 2003). Foucault may have gone slightly out of fashion, but there is an increasing tendency to (re)insert the personal into the professional via therapeutic discourses, the emphasis on mentoring, personal portfolios, reflective practice (Clegg and David, 2006) and the prominence of interpersonal and communication skills in employability discourses (Morley, 2007).

Are micropolitics morally and culturally located?

There are questions about why study micropolitics, and for what purposes can micropolitical literacy be applied (Marshall and Scribner, 1991). If micropolitcal awareness is a tool, who should use it and to what end? Whenever I lecture on the topic, students and colleagues invariably ask me if some people do and others do not engage in micropolitical activity and whether it is always negative, manipulative and oppressive or linked to particular political ideologies, identities or turf wars. Is it transgressive or regressive? I suggest that micropolitics is endemic to all organisations and that micropolitical theory recognises control and conflict as fundamental and contradictory bases of organisational life. Micropolitical activity is engaged in throughout the organisational hierarchy both to promote and to impede change. Taking the Foucauldian (1979) notion of power as both productive and oppressive, micropolitics can be regressive and conservative: for example, the mobilisation of the 'old guard' against change. Micropolitical networking and coalition-building can be also used to promote interventions for change, e.g. the curriculum development of women's and gender studies. Micropolitical interference can block interventions for change, e.g. anti-discriminatory policies. Micropolitics can be a vehicle for more generalised opposition, for radical dissent or for the assertion of minority interests and identities. Micropolitics involves constraints, limitations, frustrations, pressures opportunities of organisational membership and generates a basis for struggles, manoeuvres, bargains and alliances, through which individuals and groups compete for advantage and influence.

I am also frequently asked if I am an advocate or critic of micropolitical activity. My response is that micropolitical literacy and the ability to differentiate theory-for-understanding from theory-for-practice are important (Hoyle, 1999). An understanding of micropolitics can help to reveal the increasingly subtle and sophisticated ways in which dominance is achieved in organisations. A micropolitical perspective can shift the locus of analysis and allow one to see how power is exercised and experienced in organisations, rather than simply possessed (Morley, 1999, 2003).

I have used micropolitical theory to attempt to make sense of my gender and classed experiences and identities. It has helped me to extend my feminist understanding of the personal as political to professional and organisational contexts. What appears trivial in a single instance acquires new significance when located within a wider analysis of power relations. The attribution of meaning and decoding of transactions, locations and language are important components of micropolitics. Without wishing to sound as if I have rejected all possibility for agency, understanding micropolitics has sometimes provided me with an analytical corrective to traditional notions of disembodied objectivity and meritocracy. It has also helped me both to gain some analytical distance from bruising encounters and exclusions while also recognising that identifying one's own discomforts can provide valuable information about how wider systems of power operate.

I have also used micropolitical theory as a conceptual tool for analysing empirical data from Europe, Africa and Asia. Although I do not wish to sound evangelical, unreflexive or uncritical, I am always surprised at how well the theories travel across national and cultural boundaries. For postcolonial societies such as Nigeria, Tanzania or Uganda, or nations in the process of transition and transformation such as South Africa, micropolitical theory allows the development of new vocabularies and conceptual grammars to explain some of the frustrations of deeply sedimented power relations. Even in transformational policy arenas such as South Africa, there are questions about the extent to which aspirational interventions for redress are interpreted and resisted at local level. For those communities struggling against racial and gender oppression, bullying and sexual harassment, experiences can be subtle, elusive and volatile. Naming power relations can be a form of power, as the language in which oppressed groups describe abuses of power is often politically and socially subjugated or rendered irrelevant or illegitimate by dominant discourses.

In the nebulous world of micropolitics, what counts as evidence?

In the following sections, I would like to share some empirical data from my research projects in different national locations. To start, I will discuss the Gender Equity in Commonwealth Higher Education Project (Morley *et al.*, 2006). This study involved policy analysis, observation and interviews with over 200 staff, students and policy-makers in public universities in five countries: Nigeria, South Africa, Sri Lanka, Tanzania and Uganda. The focus was on what enabled and impeded women's access to higher education, curriculum transformation and professional development. Attention was paid to whether macro policies for gender equity such as the CEDAW (the Convention on the Elimination of All Forms of Discrimination against Women, 1979) and the Beijing Platform for Action (1995) were being implemented at meso and micro levels. Gender is explicitly on the national policy agenda in three of the five countries, i.e. South Africa, Uganda and Tanzania. The research project found that there were varying degrees of success in implementation and the relation between macro-level (national and international), meso-level (organisational and departmental) and micro-level (individuals and groups) changes was still problematic. Policy micropolitics were evident. There were frequently hidden transcripts of discrimination even in the policy contexts most committed to gender equity (Morley, 2006). South Africa had one of the most prolific policy development environments in higher education. Yet disappointment with the impact of transformation policy in South Africa has been the subject of several studies (Martineau, 1997; Ndungane, 1999; Mabokela, 2000). A South African academic in the Morley *et al.* (2006: 65) study highlighted the difference between policy intention, text and outcomes: 'there's a policy framework and we live in a wonderful democratic country which supports gender equity in so many ways but in practice we don't experience that in our daily lives'.

106

Several informants discussed the dissonance between the progressive South African policy image and identity that was being presented to the external world and the slowness of change internally – a classic public/private binary. Others discussed the micropolitics of social, interpersonal and intrapersonal relations. A feature of micropolitics is that the subtlety sometimes leaves recipients of discriminatory behaviour unsure about the accuracy of their interpretations. Recipients of discrimination can self-blame, and their uncomfortable feelings and reactions can be evidence both to themselves and to others that they are unsuited to seniority.

The development of anti-discriminatory legislation and organisational policies for equality can mean that overt displays of sexism, racism, homophobia, disablism (and what Judith Butler terms 'embarrassed etcs.' (Butler, 1999) are unlikely to be incriminatingly expressed in polite professional circles. However, discrimination can occur via informal relays of power, e.g. sarcasm, jokes, exclusions and throwaway remarks (Morley, 1999). This can make use of formal complaints or grievance procedures particularly difficult. Consequently, many experiences of discrimination remain hidden from official policy interventions such as gender mainstreaming or equal opportunities (Deem *et al.*, 2005). The nebulous nature of sexism was observed in all five locations in the Morley *et al.* (2006) study. A Nigerian woman academic commented: 'generally people believe that there is equity. But I don't think so. What now operates is done in a subtle way, so that if one complains, one looks stupid because it is so subtle. It is there, but you can't pinpoint it' (Morley *et al.* 2006: 61).

In the Cartesian dualism of mind vs body/emotion, dominant groups tend to be constructed as rational in most societies. The gendered, racialised and socially classed 'other' is usually allocated to the domain of emotions and embodiment. Hence to react against 'trivia' is evidence of lack of rationality and emotional over-sensitivity.

Informants in South Africa report how their strong national policy framework for transformation does not always get internalised and applied to evaluations of competence. Once again, a South African academic observed the slipperiness of it all, and how women appear to share a collective identity forged in difference and inferiority:

> You know it's hard to put a finger on any outright sexism that ever happens, but I think it does. I think there is, as I say that expectation that men do a better job than women and so perhaps women are not selected for committees to the same degree, perhaps not promoted to the same degree.
>
> (Morley *et al.*, 2006: 100)

Uganda has a strong policy context of gender equity, with affirmative action programmes and gender mainstreaming initiatives, supported by the international donor community. It is a signatory to major international treaties including CEDAW (1979). However, a Ugandan academic suggested that policy activity and actual practices are communicating mixed messages to women: 'The problem is how to go through the barriers. They say the doors are open, but we are still tied. They tie your hands and blindfold you then they say "the door is open". So how do you move, we are still very far.'

In this analysis, women's 'underachieving' identity can be neatly explained in terms of lack – of agency, aspiration and ability – as the structures and policy architecture are presented as enabling for women.

For many informants in the Morley *et al.* (2006) study, agency (i.e. the capacity of individuals and groups to make and impose choices and take purposive action) rather than structures (i.e. those aspects of society or organisations that place constraints on the exercise of agency, including bureaucracies, rules, laws and policies) was the explanation for women's under-representation in senior positions. A Nigerian academic argued that gendered change is related to women's individual (lack of) actions rather than to discriminatory structures:

> The thing is, there is no discrimination as per 'women must not enter this profession, woman must not do this, woman must not do that'. There is no written code or unwritten code. That's why I say the problem is the women themselves. If you feel you are up to a thing, you should go ahead and pursue it, not allowing any cultural barrier or whatever.
>
> (Morley *et al.*, 2006: 63)

A question remains as to why many women do not always put themselves forward. One explanation is that dealing with quotidian examples of sexism has a detrimental effect on women's self-confidence and career aspirations (Seymour and Hewitt, 1997; Morley, 1999). It can influence women's willingness or reluctance to attract visibility and hence their participation and engagement in leadership roles. The difficulty with attributing problems to women's psychic narratives is that it is a theory of disadvantage, rather than a theory of power and privilege. It overlooks the power relations that undermine women's confidence in their abilities. It also includes a deeply normative assumption about the signs of confidence.

As I argued earlier, micropolitical activity is engaged in by people occupying a range of organisational positions. Boundaries are often held and policed by peers. A Sri Lankan student in Morley *et al.* (2006) observed that discrimination against women often comes from micropolitical activity among students: 'I think they need to work more on changing students' attitudes. Students are so conservative and try to put down people, especially women who are doing well.'

Studies on non-decision-making (e.g. Marchbank, 2001) suggest that micropolitical activity can take the form of inaction. Creative non-implementation of progressive policies is a key micropolitical strategy to impede change. Discrimination can happen by default rather than design. The South African research team in Morley *et al.*

(2006) argued that women were not targeted negatively in their case-study organisation, but they were not actively promoted either. In South Africa, policies mention gender, language is sensitive, numbers are counted, and women are welcomed at the institution level but are then left to fend for themselves. Very few of them rose to senior positions (Shackleton *et al.*, 2005). This corresponds with research undertaken in Kenya (Onsongo, 2000) and in Finland (Husu, 2000). Both these studies highlight how there is an invitational system to apply for promotion and reveal that women are less likely to be invited than their male counterparts. In this sense, there was a complex combination of policy and management micropolitics. In the Morley *et al.* (2006) study, women staff reported that they did not feel encouraged to apply for senior management or academic posts, or to seek appropriate training to qualify them for seniority. Their gendered identities were perceived in opposition to the type of identities required for leadership. Women perceived fewer opportunities to develop professional and intellectual capital and often felt that the capital that they did possess was devalued and misrecognised in the gendered knowledge economy. Widespread favouritism of men for training and development opportunities was communicated. There were also complaints about lack of guidance, mentorship and facilitation of women's academic and management careers. Overt discrimination was reported in relation to resource allocation – particularly for professional development. Two Nigerian academics in Morley *et al.* (2006) discussed favouritism of men:

> There should be some allowance made for women to be sent on training programmes, development, staff development and all that, women should be considered, because here ... the men are given upper hand. When there are conferences to be attended, they should make it 50–50, if they need four people, two female, two male, two female members of staff, two ladies, two women.
>
> (Morley *et al.*, 2006: 100)

The above suggestion of a quota system is invariably seen as controversial as there is a strong belief that higher education is meritocratic and gender neutral (Deem *et al.*, 2005).

Affirmative action is one type of intervention for change in equity-driven political agendas. It is wide open to micropolitical interfeience. Writing in the USA, Tierney (1997) classified three positions of affirmative action: a compensatory procedure to address injustices of the past; a corrective tool to address present discrimination, and an intervention to promote social equality and diversity. Programmes tend to consist of organisational goals for increasing the representation of historically excluded groups, timetables for their achievement and the introduction of strategies and practices to support the targets (Bobo, 1998; Konrad and Hartmann, 2001). In Tanzania and Uganda affirmative action is a policy priority. While this has been perceived as contributing to increasing the quantitative representation of women students in higher education, it too has been accompanied by micropolitical interference in the form of stigmatisation and backlash. A Tanzanian academic reported damaged identities and name-calling of women students who enter via affirmative action programmes:

> First is social challenge. This is because the females entering through these programmes are dubbed names like 'VIDU — the short form of 'Viwango Duni1' (i.e. low merits), which may tend to make them feel inferior to other students and also discourage others to join the programmes.
>
> (Morley *et al.*, 2006: 76)

Affirmative action implies changes in benefit streams and the name-callers seemed to perceive it as a form of 'reverse discrimination' (Jordaan, 1995: 53). Affirmative action programmes can sometimes be seen as charity, welfare benefit or preferential treatment that automatically signifies inferiority (Fraser, 1997). Micropolitical activity sometimes leads to macro-level changes. In the USA, entire affirmative action programmes in higher education were disrupted by high-profile legal challenges from white candidates whose university applications had been rejected (Gurin *et al.*, 2002). The dominant group repositioned their identities as victims of discrimination.

Negotiating equity in higher education

Collective identities and the apparatus of micropolitics appear to have a transnational reach. Micropolitical processes described in Africa and Asia were similar to findings from a research project conducted by Rosemary Deem, Anwar Tlili and me in the UK in 2004. The research involved case studies of six HEIs, and focused on staff perceptions and reported experiences of equal opportunity policies in HEIs. Three of the sites were in England ('Towngate' HE College, 'Cityscape' University and 'Eastville' University), two in Scotland ('Speyside' University and 'Sandside' University) and one in Wales ('Westside' University). The sites were chosen to reflect a cross-section of HEIs with different missions (e.g. research intensive, research and teaching, teaching only), a variety of settings including different sizes of student intake, split sites and single sites, urban and suburban locales, and different institutional origins. Two former polytechnics or technology colleges which became universities only in 1992 (Eastville and Speyside), a college (Towngate) that was once solely focused on teacher education but now has a much wider curriculum, and three chartered or pre-1992 universities (Cityscape, Westside and Sandside) were included. Informants included vice chancellors, trade union representatives, cleaners, technicians, administrative and academic staff, from different social and cultural groups, including those who might have experience of different forms of inequality, such as staff with disabilities, gay, transgender and lesbian staff and those who belonged to ethnic and/or religious minority groups.

Like the observations in Morley *et al.* (2006), informants in Deem *et al.* (2005) reported how exclusion is often abstract and nebulous. A lesbian professor from Cityscape said:

> I think many of the stories that I've heard from other people are not about explicit anti, you know anti-gay, homophobic, where someone says, you know, I'm not promoting you because you're a queer or you're not doing this, it's much more subtle than that, and it's about people not being seen to fit in, people not looking like, their face doesn't fit. And that's never quite said to them, but they get, they get marginalised.
>
> (Deem *et al.*, 2005: 61)

Support staff at Cityscape also described how some identities converged, and others collided, with the organisational culture. Organisations can be agents of normalisation. The image of the face-not-fitting syndrome was evoked to illustrate the subtlety of organisational cultures, and favouritism, encoded in the Aryan image of the 'blue-eyed blond':

> A couple of departments will only employ blue-eyed blondes ... we had an example where a post was created for someone and the first thing ... we're in the same faculty and the first thing we knew about it was they said 'Oh so and so's been made ...' And I was one of the first people to go to the head and say 'Well how come?' you know. 'We should have internally advertised this post.' And it was a post created for this person because he was a blue-eyed boy, and that was it.
>
> (Deem *et al.*, 2005: 61)

Another way in which micropolitical sabotage can occur is via selective communication. While many informants complained of general information overload, others noted how power relations operated to stifle or withhold information. A female lecturer from Cityscape reported how male-dominated coalitions excluded her:

> The banding together of men within the department and the keeping of knowledge and information, some of which is essential to be able to do my job properly, a sort of deliberate withholding of that information when it was needed to execute a particular task, and then that being interpreted as me not knowing the systems or me not being sufficiently savvy or experienced in higher education. So there is definitely a control on the passage of information which has been used in quite a damaging way in my experience.
>
> (Deem *et al.*, 2005: 63)

Control of access to opportunities through control of access to information is a well-established micropolitical activity.

An Eastville academic informant commented on how racism is conveyed micropolitically via everyday management practices and assessments of competence, capabilities and capacity:

> You don't issue instructions, you don't micro-manage your black staff, criticise them and investigating every little thing they do, looking, fault-finding, or pretending that well you're just checking up but really what you're doing is you're saying that you're in the post but you're only there because you're black, you're not really able to do the job, I'm going to have to do everything, and of course there's the exasperation and the annoyance that goes with that. When somebody feels that they have to constantly be checking your work, they let you know that they're angry about it because they're thinking I've got to do extra work because I've got this black person sitting here.
>
> (Deem *et al.*, 2005: 63)

The racialisation of authority and collective racialised identity of lacking competence was followed through into a pattern of ethnic minority staff failing to get promotion. Three respondents, all lecturers, adduced the example of a recent promotion round where ethnic minority members of staff who, based on the stated promotion criteria, stood a very good chance of getting promoted were not even shortlisted.

One of the Eastville respondents believed discrimination due to his ethnicity might have been combined with an ageist calculation:

> Ethnic minority members of staff they are not here to expect favours from the university. Many of them, we just want a fair deal and I have the feeling that fair deal is not being given and offered to us. When I joined here ... I was taken two increments below the senior lecturer and after two years I have been, but last 24 years on the top of senior lecturer scale, did all this research and other thing and got nowhere, so there it is ... only got literally 15 months left to retirement then I shall be 65. I don't know whether ageism worked against me because if they had promoted me a few months ago I would have only left two years, whether that was factored into their calculations or their decision making process only the management can tell.
>
> (Deem *et al.*, 2005: 64)

What may reinforce the feeling of racially motivated exclusion is when there is an absence of ethnic minority staff in managerial and middle-managerial staff across the institution, a situation that has been perpetuated by what respondents saw as dubious and unclear procedures for appointment to managerial positions and allocation of managerial tasks. An Eastville respondent described the appointment of the deputy head of school:

> Why wasn't it [middle-managerial post] advertised? Here was an opportunity now for the university to appoint an ethnic minority person at that level, it was not advertised, it was just given to him ... there's not a single ethnic minority staff above the course tutorship here. Above this level there are course directors. Not a single ethnic minority person ... None of them, they're all English people. And moreover, none of them have got a PhD. Down here, course tutors ... we're all ethnic minority people with PhDs. .... The management, yes, the school, head of school, perhaps endorsed by the pro-VC ... so this is institutional racism.
>
> (Deem *et al.*, 2005: 66)

As the above instances show, the micropolitical terrain is perhaps the most challenging, the most sensitive, and the most contingent of all aspects of the conduct and implementation of equality and diversity policies. Institutional macropolicies can be sabotaged and undermined by intense subjective struggles at the micro level of the day-to-day experiences of staff, struggles over stakes and interests specific to the academic game (Bourdieu, 1988). Backstage micropolitics highlights the 'disjuncture' between cultural/normative engineering (the official formal culture that the institution's policies try to enforce) and the actual embodied and enacted norms, identities, tactics, concerns, allegiances and priorities.

Summary

Organisations, professions and management theory frequently have a rational declared set of objectives, priorities and ethics. These are often formally encoded in mission statements, guidelines and codes of practice. There is an irrational side to organisations, with informal networks, coalitions and intelligence that can promote or undermine initiatives and interventions for change. The irrationality and informality mean that it is difficult to capture, label and mobilise around issues relayed micropolitically, e.g. racism and sexism in organisations. For example, gendered processes can be open and explicit as in the case of sexual harassment or 'submerged in organisational decisions, even those that appear to have nothing to do with gender' (Mavin and Bryans, 2002: 236). Power, interests, coalitions, conflict and professional identities are intrinsically linked. Micropolitical practices can often be lagging behind, and indeed dissonant with the macro policies that aim to engineer a transformation of professional and organisational cultures. There is an affective economy in organisations and professions that can be mobilised to facilitate or impede counter-hegemonic interventions. The transnational reach of micropolitical activity reinforces the need for a global politics of difference.

References

Altrichter, H. and Salzgeber, S. (2000) 'Some elements of a micro-political theory of school development'. In H. Altrichter and J. Elliott (eds), *Images of Educational Change*. Buckingham: Open University Press.

Bacharach, S.B. and Mundell, B.L. (1993) 'Organisational politics in schools: micro, macro and logics of action'. *Educational Administration Quarterly*, 19 (4): 423–52.

Ball, S. (1987) *The Micropolitics of the School*. London: Routledge.

Ball, S. (1994) *Education Reform: A Critical and Post-Structuralist Approach*. Milton Keynes: Open University.

Benjamin, S. (2002) *The Micropolitics of Inclusive Education: An Ethnography.* Buckingham: Open University Press.

Blase, J. (1991) *The Politics of Life in Schools.* Newbury Park CA: Sage.

Blase, J. and Anderson, G. (1995) *The Micropolitics of Educational Leadership: From Control to Empowerment*. London: Cassell.

Bobo, L. (1998) 'Race, interests and beliefs about affirmative action'. *American Behavioral Scientist*, 41: 985–1003.

Bourdieu, P. (1988) *Homo Academicus.* Cambridge: Polity Press.

Budgeon, S. (2001) 'Emergent feminist(?) identities: young women and the practice of micropolitics'. *European Journal of Women's Studies*, 8 (7): 7–28.

Burns, T. (1961) 'Micropolitics: mechanisms of institutional change'. *Administrative Science Quarterly*, 6 (3): 257–81.

Butler, J.P. (1999) *Gender Trouble: Feminism and the Subversion of Identity*. New York and London: Routledge.

Clegg, S. and David, M. (2006) 'Passion, pedagogies and the project of the personal in higher education'. *Twenty First Century Society*, 1 (2): 149–65.

Deem, R., Morley, L. and Tlili, A. (2005) *Negotiating Equity in UK Universities*. London: HEFCE.

Foucault, M. (1979) *Discipline and Punish*. New York: Vintage.

Fraser, N. (1997) *Justice Interruptus: Critical Reflections On The 'Post-Socialist' Condition*. New York and London: Routledge.

Gurin, P., Dey, E., Hurtado, S. and Gurin, G. (2002) 'Diversity and higher education: theory and impact on educational outcomes'. *Harvard Educational Review*, 72 (3): 332–66.

Hearn, J. (1994) 'The organization(s) of violence: men, gender relations, organizations and violences'. *Human Relations*, 47 (6): 731–54.

Hoyle, E. (1982) 'Micro-politics of educational organisations'. *Educational Management and Administration*,10: 87–98.

Hoyle, E. (1999) 'The two faces of micropolitics'. *School Leadership & Management*, 19 (2): 213–22.

Husu, L. (2000) 'Gender discrimination in the Promised Land of gender equality'. *Higher Education in Europe*, XXV (2): 221–8.

Iannaccone, L. (1975). *Educational Policy Systems*. Fort Lauderdale FL: Nova University Press.

Jordaan, J. (1995) 'Affirmative action: excellence versus equity'. *South African Journal of Higher Education,* 9 (1): 53–64.

Kelchtermans, G. (2007) 'Macropolitics caught up in micropolitics: the case of the policy on quality control in Flanders (Belgium)'. *Journal of Education Policy*, 22 (4): 471–91.

Keltchermans, G. and Ballet, K. (2002) 'The micropolitics of teacher induction: a narrative-biographical study on teacher socialisation'. *Teaching and Teacher Education*, 18: 105–20.

Kelchtermans, G. and Ballet, K. (2003) 'Micropolitical literacy: reconstructing a neglected dimension in teacher development'. *International Journal of Educational Research*, 37: 755–67.

Konrad, A. and Hartmann, L. (2001) 'Gender differences in attitudes toward affirmative action programs in Australia: effects of beliefs, interests and attitudes toward women'. *Sex Roles*, 45 (5/6): 415–32.

Mabokela, R.O. (2000) '"We cannot find qualified blacks": faculty diversification programmes at South African universities'. *Comparative Education*, 36 (1): 95–112.

Marchbank, J. (2001) *Women, Power and Policy: Comparative Studies of Childcare.* London: Routledge.

Marshall, C. and Scribner, J. (1991) '"It's all political": inquiry into the micropolitics of education'. *Education and Urban Society*, 23: 347.

Martineau, R. (1997) 'Women and education in South Africa: factors influencing women's educational progress and their entry into traditionally male-dominated fields'. *Journal of Negro Education*, 66 (4): 383–95.

Mavin, S. and Bryans, P. (2002) 'Academic women in the UK: mainstreaming our experiences and networking for action'. *Gender and Education*, 14 (3): 235–50.

Middlehurst, R. (2000) 'Higher education professionals for the 21st century'. *Perspectives: Policy and Practice in Higher Education*, 4: 100–4.

Milliken, J. (2001) ' "Surfacing" the micropolitics as a potential change frame in higher education'. *Journal of Higher Education Policy and Management*, 23 (1): 75–84.

Morley, L. (1999). *Organising Feminisms: The Micropolitics of the Academy.* London: Macmillan.

Morley, L. (2003) *Quality and Power in Higher Education.* Buckingham: Open University Press.

Morley, L. (2005) 'The micropolitics of quality'. *Critical Quarterly*, 47 (1–2): 83–95.

Morley, L. (2006) 'Hidden transcripts: the micropolitics of gender in Commonwealth universities'. *Women's Studies International Forum*, 29 (6): 543–51.

Morley, L. (2007) 'The X factor: employability, elitism and equity in graduate recruitment'. *21st Century: Journal of The Academy of Social Sciences*, 2 (2): 191–207.

Morley, L., Gunawardena, C., Kwesiga, J., Lihamba, A., Odejide, A., Shackleton, L. and Sorhaindo, A. (2006). *Gender Equity in Selected Commonwealth Universities.* Research Report No. 65 to the Department for International Development. London: DFID.

Ndungane, P. (1999) 'Women academics in research in humanities and social sciences at universities in South Africa'. Unpublished MA dissertation, Institute of Education, University of London.

Onsongo, J. (2000) 'Publish or perish? An investigation into academic women's access to research and publication in Kenyan universities'. Unpublished MA dissertation, Institute of Education, University of London.

Paechter, C. (1995) *Crossing Subject Boundaries: The Micropolitics of Curriculum Innovation*. London: HMSO.

Reay, D. (1998) 'Micro-politics in the 1990s: staff relationships in secondary schooling'. *Journal of Education Policy*, 13 (2): 179–96.

Seymour, E. and Hewitt, N.M. (1997) *Talking About Leaving: Why Undergraduates Leave the Sciences*. Oxford: Westview Press.

Shackleton, L., Simonis, D. and Riordian, S. (2005) 'South Africa'. In *Working Paper 5: Data Analysis II*. London: Institute of Education.

Tierney, W. (1997) 'The parameters of affirmative action: equity and excellence in the academy'. *Review of Educational Research*, 67: 165–96.

7 The challenges of widening participation for professional identities and practices
Penny Jane Burke

Concepts and critiques of widening participation

This chapter considers some of the challenges of widening participation for professional identities and practice in higher educational fields. It interrogates the discourses of widening participation and the implications of these for the constitution of new professional identities and practices in a changing higher educational landscape. The chapter presents a critique of widening participation that draws on feminist poststructural perspectives. Such theoretical perspectives are concerned to expose the politics of identity and the complex ways that mis/representations, mis/recognitions and exclusions are constructed, challenged, resisted and produced (Ball, 1987, 1990; Fraser, 1997; Skeggs, 1997, 2004; Gillborn and Youdell, 2000; Reay, 2001; Epstein *et al.*, 2003; Reay *et al.*, 2005). These theoretical insights and critiques will help to think through the implications of widening participation for professional identities and practices in higher education.

Although widening participation (WP) has become a key policy discourse with particular orientations since the New Labour Government came into power in 1997, the project to widen access and participation in higher education has a long history, with competing perspectives and approaches. Within these competing perspectives, there has been a strong commitment to redress the structural inequalities in higher education by targeting historically under-represented groups and developing support mechanisms to increase their participation in higher education. Access to higher education courses in England were initially developed with such aims in mind and there was a clear strand of social justice running through this project (Kirton, 1999; Burke, 2002). Similarly, in the US, a radical tradition exists whereby affirmative action policies were put into place to redress unequal participation patterns across different social groups and to encourage, in particular, the participation of black students in higher education (Allen *et al.*, 2005).

Jones and Thomas (2005) outline three contrasting approaches to WP. The first they categorise as the 'academic approach'. This strand emphasises attitudinal factors such as 'low aspirations'. In this approach, activities to raise aspirations are prioritised and these are located at the peripheries of universities with 'little or no impact on institutional structure and culture' (Jones and Thomas, 2005: 617). The second approach that they outline is the 'utilitarian approach' which also focuses on attitudinal factors as well as lack of academic qualifications. Jones and Thomas characterise this approach as the 'double deficit model' (Jones and Thomas, 2005: 618) and one that particularly emphasises the relationship between higher education and the economy. The third approach they name 'transformative' which focuses on the needs of under-represented groups in higher education. They argue that higher-status institutions are more likely to take the academic approach, less prestigious institutions are more likely to take the utilitarian approach, leaving little space for transformative approaches to higher education (Jones and Thomas, 2005: 627).

In England, as most 'non-traditional' entrants to higher education are concentrated in the post-1992 new universities, the hegemonic discourse of widening participation is strongly framed by the utilitarian approach and the 'logic of neo-liberal globalisation' (Jones *et al.*, 1999: 238). Within this context, there is a firm acceptance that the economy and marketplace are at the centre of the project to widen participation as a key policy imperative. With notions of the market at the centre of WP policy, the key role of HE is constructed as enhancing employability, entrepreneurialism, economic competitiveness and flexibility (Morley, 1999; Thompson, 2000; Burke, 2002; Archer *et al.*, 2003; Bowl, 2003). Neo-liberal market-oriented approaches characterise WP activities (Burke and Jackson, 2007).

Neo-liberalism attempts to erase issues of social identity and inequality and positions individual students as 'consumers' of, and equal players in, the free market of higher education. Sociologists argue that WP tends to operate around contradictory claims; on the one hand, the claim of the 'classless society' or the 'death of class' and, on the other, the powerful ways that 'class is invoked in moves to draw young people from deprived areas into HE' (Lawler, 2005: 798). In similar ways, issues of gender equality are often seen as irrelevant in WP policy debates but reappear as a national concern in relation to the perceived crisis of masculinity and the claim that women are taking over the university (Quinn, 2003). WP policy is a part of the broader technologies of self-regulation in which subjects come to understand themselves as responsible for the production of a self with the skills and qualities required to succeed in the new economy (Walkerdine, 2003: 239). Issues of structural inequality and cultural misrecognition become hidden in WP policy discourse, and rather individuals are called upon to take up the challenge of WP. Such a challenge is located in a wider neo-liberal project of self-development and improvement through participation in lifelong learning opportunities, which are presented as meritocratic and available to all who have the potential to benefit. Within this framework, new professional roles have been developed specifically to take forward the WP agenda within the utilitarian framework outlined above.

However, this is not to say that discourses of transformation and social justice are not still at play to some extent in WP policy, as this quote from the Higher Education Funding Council for England (HEFCE) demonstrates:

> Widening participation addresses the large discrepancies in the take-up of higher education opportunities between different social groups. Under-representation is closely connected with broader issues of equity and social inclusion, so we are concerned with ensuring equality of opportunity for disabled students, mature students, women and men, and all ethnic groups.

(HEFCE, 2008)

The problematic of this excerpt becomes apparent though with close analytical attention to the framing policy text, which places emphasis on individuals from under-represented groups taking responsibility to change their aspirations, dispositions and values (Gerwirtz, 2001). This has significantly altered relations between the individual and the state and has led to a shift from government to governance, 'signalling a move away from a citizen-based notion of rights associated with a sense of the public, to an individualistic client-based notion of right based on contractual obligations' (Blackmore, 2006: 13). WP professionals are expected to support individuals with potential from disadvantaged backgrounds in raising their aspirations. I have argued elsewhere that aspirations are not individually formed but are relational and interconnected with complex auto/biographies, multiple identities and social positionings and are discursively produced within schools, colleges and universities (Burke, 2006). What is not considered in the hegemonic discourses of WP is the necessity of transforming education institutions in order to seriously address deeply embedded structural inequalities and discursive misrecognitions across intersections of age, class, dis/ability, ethnicity, gender, inter/nationality, race, religion and sexuality. These complex inequalities are intricately intertwined with longstanding cultural and discursive mis/representations, which produce discourses of derision (Ball, 1990) and pathologised subjectivities (Skeggs, 2004). In critiquing what she names as the narrow skills-driven approach to WP policies, Carole Leathwood warns that such policies are likely to fail if they refuse to engage with the complex reasons that different social groups might be resistant to education in relation to their negative experiences of learning in formal institutions:

> The current lifelong learning strategy is likely to fail if the narrow skills-driven approach which alienates potential learners continues to be pursued. There is already a healthy resistance to participation from many who regard the education on offer as middle-class and alien, and without any attempts to address the reasons for such resistance, and to ensure that educational opportunities offer positive and relevant experiences and benefits, many of those who are intended recipients of lifelong learning are likely to continue to resist it.
>
> (Leathwood, 2006: 52)

Indeed, those entering higher education from 'different' backgrounds are often seen as potentially contaminating university standards and, as a result, a key policy strategy is to protect the quality of higher education by creating new and different spaces for those new and different students (Morley, 2003). For example the Government White Paper, *The Future of Higher Education*, reads:

> Our overriding priority is to ensure that as we expand HE places, we ensure that the expansion is of an appropriate quality and type to meet the demands of employers and the needs of the economy and students. We believe that the economy needs more work focused degrees – those, like our new foundation degrees, that offer specific, job-related skills. We want to see expansion in two-year, work-focused foundation degrees; and in mature students in the workforce developing their skills. As we do this, we will maintain the quality standards required for access to university, both *safeguarding the standards of traditional honours degrees and promoting a step-change in the quality and reputation of workfocused courses*.
>
> (DfES, 2003: 64, emphasis added)

In this excerpt, WP is being explicitly linked with concerns about 'safeguarding the standards of traditional honours degrees'. The text implies that opening access to new student constituencies has the potential to have a negative effect on traditional university spaces, which need to be protected against the entry of 'non-traditional' students. It also assumes that the appropriate level of participation for those new student constituencies is work-based degrees rather than traditional honours degrees. This leads policy in the direction of creating new and different kinds of courses for new and different kinds of students without addressing that these differences are shown to be classed, gendered and racialised by research in the field (HEFCE, 2005; Reay *et al.*, 2005). In this way, the WP policy agenda is not able to challenge the status quo or redress the legacy of the under-representation of certain social groups in traditional forms of higher education, which carry with them status and esteem. As a result, enduring hierarchies, privileges and inequalities remain untouched while new forms of unequal social relations are being created (Burke, 2002). This logic constructs 'WP students' in very particular ways and leaves notions of deficit in place. Traditional student identity is subtly held in place so that the traditional university undergraduate is reconstituted as white-racialised and middle-classed. The 'WP student' is constituted as 'Other', deserving of higher education access but only to 'other' kinds of courses and institutions.

Widening participation and professional identities in higher education

The majority of literature on professional identity in higher education focuses on academic identities (e.g. Henkel, 2000; Anderson and Williams, 2001; Morley, 2003). This literature is concerned to understand the impact of a changing higher educational landscape on conceptualising academic identity and notions of professionalism.

> Higher education is undergoing a series of complex overlapping changes, which are profoundly affecting its organisational structures, traditional practices, and the way in which its institutions and those who work within them are viewed by the public.
>
> (Nixon *et al.*, 2001: 229)

Nixon *et al.* (2001) outline the literature on professionalism and higher education, which presents a crisis of professional identity in universities as a result of expansion, new managerialism, increasingly diverse practices, lack of autonomy and self-regulation and alternative values and aspirations (Nixon *et al.*, 2001: 231). They present an alternative conceptualisation of professionalism in the following ways:

> It sees professionalism as the capacity of an occupational group to be extrovert, generous and knowledgeable in its relations with professional colleagues, other professional groups, and 'the public'. It defines professionalism, therefore, not in terms of status and self-regulation, but in terms of values and practices. Why I do what I do is of the utmost significance; as are the deliberative processes whereby I address that 'why'. Without this emphasis on the moral purposefulness of practice, there would be no claim to professionalism
>
> (Nixon *et al.*, 2001: 234).

Clearly the emphasis on values and practices is significant and important in the context of WP. Indeed, a transformative approach to widening participation would place strong emphasis on the ways that academic practices (in relation to curriculum, assessment, pedagogy and quality assurance for example) are tied up with the values, epistemologies and perspectives of hegemonic groups (e.g. middle class, white-racialised and (hetero)masculinised). However, I would argue this concept of professionalism does not go far enough; there is no explicit analysis of the power relations and inequalities and how these operate within the complex and subtle micropolitics of higher educational organisations (Morley, 1999; Burke and Jackson, 2007).

Furthermore, little attention has been paid to the production of new professional identities in higher education as part of the WP market. There are a range of new professional roles within and outside higher education as a result of the agenda, including the WP officer, the WP director, the head of WP, and the Aimhigher officer, among others. At the time of writing, I could not locate any statistical data to understand the size and constitution of this new professional body and the ways that these workers themselves might be constructed as 'non-traditional' and even marginal in academic spaces. Indeed, as Jones and Thomas argue in terms of utilitarian approaches, WP staff themselves tend to work on the periphery of universities, in separate centres and outside academic faculties and departments.

> Subsequently, widening participation initiatives in utilitarian influenced higher education institutions are more or less 'bolted on' to core work, for example mentoring and guidance activities, learning support mechanisms (via 'study skills centres', etc.) and stand-alone student services (Layer *et al.*, 2003). Whilst research examining student services has identified some examples of integrated student support, many student service departments reported institutional resistance to their integration into core activity (Thomas *et al.*, 2003).
>
> (Jones and Thomas, 2005: 618)

We need both quantitative and qualitative data to help us to understand the constitution of this new professional workforce, their location in the academy and their experiences of being on the front line of WP strategies. Research needs to be conducted, drawing on both quantitative and qualitative methodologies, to better understand the location of this new workforce in universities and the impact of their positioning on the approaches being taken to widening participation in higher education. For example, what are the gender relations at play within the context of this new workforce? Indeed, the deficit discourse of widening participation constructs 'WP students' as having special needs, and needing additional pastoral care (Bowl, 2003; Burke and Hermerschmidt, 2005; Burke and Jackson, 2007). It would be interesting to have data on the gender of the HE staff undertaking the majority of this additional pastoral care and whether or not it relies on the emotional labour (Hochschild, 1983) of women in particular (Burke and Jackson, 2007).

What we do know is that, in the main, those who are explicitly part of WP teams in higher education are non-academic staff and this has implications for the ways in which they are constructed within university sites. Complex power relations are at play within universities, which are intensely hierarchical institutions, although of course this plays out in different ways across a highly differentiated higher education system. WP professionals within education have primary responsibility for developing and sustaining WP strategies within their institutions and in this way WP has its own special space, outside the main work of academics.

Clegg (2005) argues that newer forms of knowledge are emerging in higher education as a result of the different career trajectories and identities that are being brought into universities: 'While universities have traditionally sustained disciplinary ways of knowing, it may be that newer ways of knowing are breaking down traditional assumptions in some areas of universities' (Clegg, 2005: 24).

It would be useful to understand more clearly the different forms of knowledge that WP professionals bring to higher education and the impact of that on the cultures, values and practices within different organisational spaces. In my own professional work, I have designed a module on widening participation. This I understand as part of my personal project to bring theory and practice more explicitly together and to explore the potential of using critical sociological tools to transform practice and to expose complex structural inequalities and discursive misrecognitions. It is also useful to open up spaces of dialogue between practitioners and researchers to refine theoretical perspectives in response to the challenges and realities of everyday practice and professional knowledge and experience. The module is entering its fifth year and each year we have on average 15 WP professionals participating on the module. Each year I have been struck by the strong sense of a lack of authority that the module participants express when they are talking about their experiences of effecting change in the institutions where they work. They often refer to their experience of not being taken seriously within their professional settings, particularly because of their 'non-academic' status. A common purpose for taking part in the module is that they want to find an (academic) language/discourse that would allow their perspectives to be taken seriously by their colleagues, particularly their academic colleagues.

It is not surprising that each year the majority of module participants are women. Higher education research has argued that complex gender inequalities continue to be at play within universities, and hegemonic constructions of femininity often undermine the authority and status of female staff (Currie *et al.*, 2002). However, in considering the complex dynamics of social inequalities, it is also important to pay attention to the ways that gender intersects with class and race. Indeed, most of the women participating on the module are white although many come from working-class backgrounds and were 'non-traditional' students themselves, exacerbating their lack of status and authority within their institutions. The point I am trying to make here is that the (multiple, fluid) identities of the new WP professional workforce matter and impact on decision-making processes, including the potential for serious questioning of what WP is, questions such as: what do we mean by widening participation? What are the implications of being constructed as a WP student? Who is responsible for WP and what are the implications for this? How is WP related to other key issues such as quality assurance/ enhancement and issues of equality and diversity? How is WP related to academic practices in higher education such as pedagogy, curriculum and assessment? Questions of identity matter as well in terms of power relations within institutions and the constructions of (lack of) authority that might facilitate or impede processes of change and transformation.

Aiming higher and raising aspirations

In this section, I interrogate the hegemonic policy discourse of 'raising aspirations', which forms a significant aspect of widening participation activities. I will deconstruct this discourse to unearth the assumptions and values underpinning it and to identify its implications for professional identities and practices in the context of WP.

Aimhigher is the key UK policy initiative to work towards New Labour's goal of increasing participation levels in higher education towards 50 per cent of 18–30-year-olds by the year 2010. This initiative aims to 'raise the aspirations' of talented individuals from disadvantaged socioeconomic backgrounds. Aimhigher undoubtedly makes a valuable contribution to WP, for example by providing useful and accessible information to parents and pupils to help them make important decisions about their future studies. However, the hegemonic discourse of 'raising aspirations' which underpins the Aimhigher framework is problematic in the ways that it contributes to the productions of deficit constructions of 'disadvantaged' communities and conceptualises aspirations as individual and linear. It is primarily located in the academic and utilitarian approach that Jones and Thomas (2005) outline, rather than the transformative approach to WP.

The main work of Aimhigher staff is seen as 'raising the aspirations' of young people who stand out as having special talent and potential despite their social positioning. The discourse locates problems of deficit in individuals, families and communities who are pathologised through the discourse of 'social exclusion' (Gerwirtz, 2001). The problem lies in the processes of identifying who has potential – and who does not – and the assumption is that such processes, if approached in a professional way, are objective and fair and unconnected from wider social inequalities. Gillborn and Youdell demonstrate in their study that the construction of ability within schools continues to be a highly classed, gendered and racialised process despite the professionalism of teachers who are implicated in the production of 'ability' (Gillborn and Youdell, 2000). The notion of 'potential' is highly subjective and rests on assumptions about ability and on privileged ontological dispositions (i.e. those coded as middle-class, white, masculine and heterosexual). Raising aspirations is constructed as an individual self-improvement project, facilitated by the new WP labour force, which occurs outside social relations and the micropolitics of educational organisations. Within this framework, the complex social and personal histories in which particular forms of knowledge and capital have been privileged and particular bodies have been coded as knowledgeable are ignored. Rather, knowledge and knowing is constructed as objective, apolitical and detached from the legacy of the misrecognition of the cultural capital, literacy practices and knowledge of historically marginalised groups (Apple, 2006).

Raising aspirations is connected to the New Labour policy discourse of social exclusion, which has been critiqued by sociologists to expose the ways that it leaves the operations of power unexamined. Shifting the attention to 'exclusion', and away from structural inequalities and discursive misrecognitions, operates as a mechanism to reprivilege particular cultural practices and values. The heterogeneity of British society is framed in terms of 'diversity' and yet the complex differences and inequalities behind diversity are silenced. This valorises particular classed, gendered and racialised dispositions, capital and identities without paying close attention to the subtle and intricate ways that power, prestige and hegemony play out to the disadvantage of certain social groups. The policy discourse of social exclusion locates the problem in individuals rather than educational systems that are reproductive of social inequalities. Importantly, sociological work emphasises that identities are produced within the discursive sites and practices of schools, colleges and universities (Mac an Ghaill, 1994). Excluded identities themselves are constructed, performed and named within schools and universities (Youdell, 2006). The emphasis on individual aspirations misses out the significant interconnections between a subject's aspirations and their classed, racialised, (hetero)sexualised and gendered identities, ignoring the social and cultural contexts in which certain subjects are constructed, and construct themselves, as having or not having potential or indeed not choosing to participate in higher education for a range of valid reasons (Archer and Leathwood, 2003). Aspirations themselves are formed through social relations and identity positions, and are negotiated and renegotiated within the social contexts where the individual is situated; they are not linear in formation but cyclical and reflexive (Burke, 2006).

WP professionals are implicated in the assumptions underpinning the discourse of raising aspirations as they are the individuals granted the responsibility for developing 'activities' that are expected to have the effect of raising aspirations. The fact that the activities are developed without serious attention to the histories and biographies of structural inequalities and discursive misrecognitions leaves the WP professional unable to intervene in any systematic way with the power relations at play in schools, colleges and universities. Instead, the role of the WP professional is to work closely with schools and teachers to identify individual students deemed to be 'disadvantaged' but 'with potential' and to provide opportunities to help them to recognise the value of participation in higher education. The possibility that judgements about who has 'potential' are interconnected with complex subjectivities and hegemonic discourses is not explored. In this context, it is unsurprising that individual WP professionals participating on my module often express a sense of frustration in their work and want to develop richer and deeper understandings of the ways that educational exclusions and inclusions operate.

The implications of these critiques for professional development and practice

I have drawn attention in this chapter to the significance of structural inequalities and cultural misrecognitions in relation to professional identities and practices of WP. Complex, multiple and shifting identities, produced within educational sites, have been put at the centre of consideration. This is in the context of WP policy which privileges the market and tends to ignore issues of identity, difference and inequality. Furthermore, I have argued that the onus of WP rests mainly on those new WP professionals who often lack status, authority and power within the universities in which they work. This is highly problematic in a context where WP is often treated as a separate issue rather than integrated into the development of professional practices across the university. Academic practices themselves are rarely interrogated in relation to issues of multiple and complex social exclusions (Burke and Hermerschmidt, 2005; Burke and Jackson, 2007) and this I argue is highly problematic for WP and those given responsibility for it.

It is important of course to note that not only are *student* identities constituted in complex and multiple ways that are always intimately interconnected with wider social and power relations across age, class, dis/ability, gender, ethnicity, nationality, race, religion, sexuality and race: so too are *professional* identities. Burke and Jackson aim to illuminate through fictional narratives the complicated ways that inequalities and misrecognitions are produced and how these are tied in with complex identities, resistances and subjectivities (Burke and Jackson, 2007). WP professionals therefore are constituted in relation to the ways that their bodies are read (in terms of age, race and gender for example) and their identities discursively produced, but also in relation to the discourses of WP itself. The politics of WP are contradictory and complex – on one hand universities are being regulated in terms of their WP strategies, yet on the other institutions are derided on the basis of their 'non-traditional' courses and students. The following quote from Margaret Hodge in 2003, who at the time was the Minister of State for Lifelong Learning and Higher Education, is an example of the discursive slippages between enthusiasm for the importance of courses that aim to widen participation, while implying the low quality of those courses and their threat to the maintenance of the highest-achieving graduates:

> Britain needs more graduates in a mass higher education system, but we also need to maintain a cohort of the most high achieving graduates who will fuel our future growth and prosperity. And that is where diversity and specialization come into their own. Universities must have diverse missions if they are to meet the workforce needs of the future. Some will continue to teach traditional subjects – although we will expect them to become more inclusive in their intake. But most of the expansion of places will need to come from vocational degrees offered in both further education and higher education institutions or through collaboration of the two sectors. What we are looking for is an expansion of foundation degrees ... At the same time simply stacking up numbers on Mickey Mouse courses is not acceptable.
>
> (quoted in Leathwood, 2007)

This quote also highlights that being connected to WP activities has implications not only for 'non-academic staff' with specific WP roles but also for 'academic staff' who work on those courses and institutions seen as relating directly to the WP agenda. This has serious career consequences for those who devote time and energy to issues of access and participation in universities. Morley explains that 'research productivity is the main criterion for academic career success' (Morley, 2003: 28). The divide between teaching and research has received dedicated attention from researchers in the field of higher education and it has been widely argued that research remains more valued in higher education than teaching (Gibbs, 1995; Coate *et al.*, 2001; Morley, 2003). This operates at an institutional as well as an individual level; English universities with the highest esteem are those recognised as 'research-intensive universities' and those rating highly in the RAE. Morley argues that the 'stratification of institutions has become more visible and more precisely differentiated' (Morley, 2003). This affects the professional identities of those working within a highly differentiated university system, and those who are connected with 'WP institutions' are constructed in a different way from those associated with prestigious traditional universities. Those who dedicate their time and energy to teaching, tutoring and pastoral care are less likely to be recognised as serious academics and to be promoted and this is gendered (Currie *et al.*, 2002), as supported by the current statistic that there are almost six full-time male professors for every female professor (BBC, 2007).

Furthermore, WP is about participation in higher education and not simply about access at the level of entry (Burke, 2006). In other words, academic practices are crucial to concerns to widen participation, including, for example, pedagogical practices. This must go beyond individualist interventions, such as a concern with 'learning styles', to attention to pedagogical relations, the politics of identity, and struggles over what counts as legitimate knowledge and ways of knowing (Burke and Jackson, 2007). Taken-for-granted practices in HE are social practices that are tied to struggles over meaning and identity – who 'knows' and what kind of knowledge counts. There is a need therefore to interrogate taken-for-granted assumptions that underpin academic practices and to develop reflexive practices that challenge neo-liberal technologies of self-regulation (Walkerdine, 2003). Rather, a critical reflexive approach would involve professionals in exploring the different and multiple social positioning they occupy, the identities they bring to their work and the judgements they make about themselves and others. Such an approach requires critical attention to the operation of power in educational contexts and this must involve those occupying high-status and powerful positions, both within universities and in national policy-making contexts.

In acknowledging the points made in this chapter then, which highlight the ways that power is exercised in intensely hierarchical institutions such as universities, the dilemma for a transformative approach to widening participation emerges. Indeed, in taking seriously the analysis presented here and by other researchers committed to social justice and inclusion in higher education (Stuart, 2000; Thompson, 2000; Anderson and Williams, 2001; Archer *et al.*, 2003; Jones and Thomas, 2005), how can those committed to a transformative project of widening participation help to shift practices away from the academic and utilitarian approaches currently prioritised in policy and practice? If those who occupy positions of authority and power in relation to setting the framework and making key decisions reprivilege discourses of utilitarianism and deficit, then how can we expect to move away from such approaches?

It is paramount that the difference between *increasing* participation and *widening* participation is understood (Archer *et al.*, 2003). Critical understandings that draw on sociological, feminist, anti-racist, postcolonial and queer theories are imperative to developing counter-hegemonic practices that might begin to destabilise privilege and inequality in higher education. Professional development needs to embrace such insights in developing programmes to support WP professionals in their work, giving them a language and a set of tools to expose subtle, insidious and almost invisible workings of power and privilege. However, it is not just about developing the understanding and resources available to WP professionals. It is about transforming academic cultures and practices so that different forms of knowledge and different kinds of learners and knowers can be recognised and validated in higher educational spaces. It is about redressing historical misrecognitions that have led to the privileging of particular epistemological frameworks in higher education (Gordon, 2007).

We need more attention on supporting the development of inclusive practices in higher education. In relation to this, it is important to interrogate taken-for-granted assumptions around 'quality' that are often in tension with issues of equality (Morley, 2003; Burke and Jackson, 2007). This requires a different approach to accountability – one that puts issues of power, inequality and misrecognition at the centre of attention. Jill Gordon argues in the context of racialised exclusions in higher education curriculum that:

> All of us, regardless of credentials, regardless of time since receiving advanced degrees or prominence in our respective fields, have an obligation to educate ourselves about the world around us, about developments in our fields, and most especially about people, events, and ideas about which our class, race and/or social position would normally insulate us from knowing. ... earning an advanced degree and entering a profession in the academy is still predominately the province of Whites who come from privileged backgrounds. ... Primarily, the obligation to educate ourselves means going out to meet the world, and not expecting it to come to us – or, perhaps more pointedly, not assuming that was has come to us constitute 'the world'.
>
> (Gordon, 2007: 339)

Gordon's words are important to understanding the complicated nature of power and responsibility in the project to widen participation in higher education. If we are to embrace inclusive and reflexive practices within higher education institutions, WP must reach beyond those in posts with explicit WP responsibility. As Burke and Jackson argue (2007), we need to enrich and broaden our concepts of 'quality' and 'accountability' to hold those in positions of status, authority and power within universities accountable to issues of equality and inclusion. This requires a *transformative* approach to widening participation, which pays careful attention to the subtle ways that the relations, practices and cultures within universities might serve to perpetuate deep-seated and historical exclusions.

References

Allen, W. R., Jayakumar, U. M., Griffen, K. A., Korn, W. S. and Hurtado, S. (2005) *Black Undergraduates from Bakke to Grutter: Freshmen Status, Trends and Prospects, 1971–2004.* Los Angeles CA: Higher Education Research Institute, University of California, Los Angeles.

Anderson, P. and Williams, J. (2001) *Identity and Difference in Higher Education: 'Outsiders Within'.* Aldershot: Ashgate.

Apple, M.W. (2006) *Educating the 'Right' Way: Markets, Standards, God, and Inequality.* London: Routledge.

Archer, L., Hutchings, M. and Ross, A. (2003) 'Widening participation in higher education: Implications for policy and practice'. In L. Archer, M. Hutchings and A. Ross (eds), *Higher Education and Social Class: Issues of Exclusion and Inclusion.* London: Routledge Falmer.

Archer, L. and Leathwood, C. (2003) 'Identities, inequalities and higher education'. In L. Archer, M. Hutchings and A. Ross (eds), *Higher Education and Social Class: Issues of Exclusion and Inclusion.* London: Routledge Falmer.

Ball, S. (1987) *The Micro-Politics of the School.* London: Methuen.

Ball, S. (1990) *Politics and Policy Making in Education.* London: Routledge.

BBC (2007) *Male Professors Outnumber Women.* Online. <http://news.bbc.co.uk/go/pr/fr/-/1/hi/education/6653705.stm.> (accessed 8 October 2007).

Blackmore, J. (2006) 'Unprotected participation in lifelong learning and the politics of hope: a feminist reality check of discourses around flexibility, seamlessness and learner earners'. In C. Leathwood and B. Francis (eds), *Gender and Lifelong Learning: Critical Feminist Engagements*. London: Routledge.

Bowl, M. (2003) *Non-Traditional Entrants to Higher Education: 'They Talk about People like Me'*. Stoke-on-Trent: Trentham Books.

Burke, P.J. (2002) *Accessing Education Effectively Widening Participation*. Stoke-on-Trent: Trentham Books.

Burke, P.J. (2006) 'Men accessing education: gendered Aspiration'. *British Educational Research Journal*, 32 (5): 719–34.

Burke, P.J. and Hermerschmidt, M. (2005) 'Deconstructing academic practices through self-reflexive pedagogies'. In B. Street (ed.), *Literacies Across Educational Contexts: Mediating Learning and Teaching*. Philadelphia PA: Caslon Press.

Burke, P.J. and Jackson, S. (2007) *Reconceptualising Lifelong Learning*. London: Routledge.

Clegg, S. (2005) *Academic Identities Under Threat?* Edinburgh: SHRE.

Coate, K., Barnett, R. and Williams, G. (2001) 'Relationships between teaching and research in higher education in England'. *Higher Education Quarterly*, 55 (2): 158–74.

Currie, J., Thiele, B. and Harris, P. (2002) *Gendered Universities in Globalized Economies: Power, Careers and Sacrifices*. Lanham BO: Lexington Books.

DfES (2003) *The Future of Higher Education*. London: DfES.

Epstein, D., O'Flynn, S. and Telford, D. (2003) *Silenced Sexualities in Schools and Universities*. Stoke-on-Trent: Trentham Books.

Fraser, N. (1997) *Justice Interruptus: Critical Reflections on the 'Postsocialist' Condition*. London: Routledge.

Gerwirtz, S. (2001) 'Cloning the Blairs: New Labour's programme for the re-socialization of working-class parents'. *Journal of Educational Policy*, 16 (4): 365–78.

Gibbs, G. (1995) 'The relationship between quality in research and quality in teaching'. *Quality in Higher Education*, 1 (2): 147–57.

Gillborn, D. and Youdell, D. (2000) *Rationing education: Policy, Practice, Reform and Equity*. Buckingham: Open University Press.

Gordon, J. (2007) 'What can White faculty do?', *Teaching in Higher Education*, 12 (3): 337–48.

HEFCE (2005) *Young Participation in Higher Education*. Bristol: Higher Education Funding Council for England.

HEFCE (2006) *Widening Participation*. Bristol: Higher Education Funding Council for England.

HEFCE (2008) *Widening Participation*. Online. <www.hefce.ac.uk/widen/> (accessed 24 April 2008).

Henkel, M. (2000) *Academic Identities and Policy Changes in Higher Education*. London: Jessica Kingsley Publishers.

Hochschild, A.R. (1983) *The Managed Heart: The Commercialization of Human Feeling*. Berkeley CA: University of California Press.

Jones, C., Turner, J. and Street, B, (1999) 'Introduction'. In C. Jones, J. Turner and B. Street (eds), *Students Writing in the University: Cultural and Epistemological Issues*. Philadelphia PA: John Benjamins Publishing Company.

Jones, R. and Thomas, L. (2005) 'The 2003 UK Government higher education White Paper: a critical assessment of its implications for the access and widening participation agenda'. *Journal of Education Policy*, 20 (5): 615–30.

Kirton, A. (1999) 'Lessons from access education'. In A. Hayton (ed.), *Tackling Disaffection and Social Exclusion: Education Perspectives and Policies*. London: Kogan Page.

Lawler, S. (2005) 'Introduction: class, culture and identity'. *Sociology*, 39 (5): 797–806.

Layer, G., Srivastava, A., Thomas, L. and Yorke, M. (2003) 'Student success: building for change'. In Action on Access (ed.), Student Success in Higher Education. Bradford: Action on Access.

Leathwood, C. (2006) 'Gendered constructions of lifelong learning and the learner in the UK policy context.' In C. Leathwood and B. Francis (eds), *Gender and Lifelong Learning: Critical Feminist Engagements*. London: Routledge.

Leathwood, C. (2007) *Widening Participation Policy*. Unpaginated module handout. London: Institute of Education .

Mac an Ghaill, M. (1994) *The Making of Men: Masculinities, Sexualities and Schooling*. Buckingham and Philadelphia: Open University Press.

Morley, L. (1999) *Organising Feminisms: The Micropolitics of the Academy*. Basingstoke: Macmillan Press.

Morley, L. (2003) *Quality and Power in Higher Education*. Maidenhead: Society for Research in Higher Education and Open University Press.

Nixon, J., Marks, A., Rowland, S. and Walker, M. (2001) 'Towards a new academic professionalism: a manifesto of hope'. *British Journal of Sociology of Education*, 22 (2): 227–44.

Quinn, J. (2003) *Powerful Subjects: Are Women Really Taking over the University?* Stoke-on-Trent: Trentham Books.

Reay, D. (2001) 'Finding or losing yourself? Working-class relationships to education'. *Journal of Education Policy*, 16 (4): 333–46.

Reay, D., David, M. and Ball, S. (2005) *Degrees of Choice: Class, Race, Gender and Higher Education*. Stoke-on-Trent: Trentham Books.

Skeggs, B. (1997) *Formations of Class and Gender: Becoming Respectable*. London: Sage.

Skeggs, B. (2004) *Class, Self, Culture*. London and New York: Routledge.

Stuart, M. (2000) 'Beyond rhetoric: reclaiming a radical agenda for active participation in higher education'. In J. Thompson (ed.), *Stretching the Academy: The Politics and Practice of Widening Participation in Higher Education*. Leicester: NIACE.

Thomas, E., Quinn, J., Slack, K. and Casey, L. (2003) *Student Services: Effective Approaches to Retaining Students in Higher Education*. Full Research Report. Stoke-on-Trent: Staffordshire University Institute for Access Studies.

Thompson, J. (2000) Introduction. In J. Thompson (ed.), *Stretching the Academy: The Politics and Practice of Widening Participation in Higher Education*. Leicester: NIACE.

Walkerdine, V. (2003) 'Reclassifying upward mobility: femininity and the neo-liberal subject'. *Gender and Education*, 15 (3): 237–49.

Youdell, D. (2006) *Impossible Bodies, Impossible Selves: Exclusions and Student Subjectivities.* Dordrecht: Springer.

8   The imaginative professional
Sally Power

The objective of this chapter is to persuade readers that the best way of confronting the contemporary challenges of professional life is to develop something called a 'professional imagination'. Borrowing from the sociology of C. Wright Mills, it argues that the development of a professional imagination will enable professionals to gauge a sense of their own efficacy within contemporary settings without resorting either to an over-individualised or to an over-determined position. Without such an imagination, professionals will be doomed to stumble from one crisis to another with little hope of illumination.

Contemporary challenges to professionalism

It is now widely accepted that the conventional conceptualisation of professionalism is no longer adequate. Traditionally, it was held that being a professional implied membership of an occupational group that could be distinguished from other (usually lesser) occupational groups on the basis of a number of characteristics. Millerson (1964), for example, examined the literature and identified 23 elements used to describe a 'profession'. These include skill based on theoretical knowledge, trust-based client relationship, adherence to a professional code of conduct, independence and altruism.

Defining professionalism along these lines, though, has been severely critiqued. For example, it can be shown that professions have developed in different ways in different societies. Rather than having universal characteristics, the history and properties of professions are historically and geographically contingent (Siegrist, 1994). The conventional definition is actually based on highly specific and idealised representations of the 'classic' professions of medicine, clergy and the law in the UK. As Witz (1990: 675) argues, 'it takes what are in fact the successful professional projects of class-privileged male actors at a particular point in history and in particular societies to be the paradigmatic case of profession'. In order to accommodate other occupational groups within the umbrella of the professions, it has been necessary to develop the categories of 'semi-' or 'quasi-professionals'.

However, even if we broaden the definition of the professions to encompass the diversity of groupings who claim such status, this idealised representation bears little resemblance to the day-to-day experiences of professionals. Many of us, perhaps particularly (but not exclusively) those of us working in the public sector, feel beleaguered – pressured by unreasonable demands from above and below, subjected to constant surveillance through 'user' evaluations, inspections and audits, constrained by risk management yet fearful of litigation. In short, it might be argued that the concept of a public-sector professional is currently a contradiction in terms. Most health professionals, social workers and teachers would certainly find it difficult to characterise their working lives in terms of those characteristics identified by Millerson, such as trust-based relationships or independence.

In confronting the difficulties of being a contemporary professional, there are three broad perspectives that can be developed. The first, which I shall call the 'therapeutic perspective', interprets the challenges (and identifies the remedies) in terms of individual and/or institutional failings. The second, which I shall call the 'deterministic perspective', interprets the difficulties in terms of structural forces beyond the individual or the institution. The third perspective, which is the most fruitful, recognises the complex relationship between individual, institution and broader society. Using the concepts developed by C. Wright Mills, I aim to show how the development of a sociological imagination can transfer to the development of a professional imagination.

The distressed professional: a therapeutic perspective

The therapeutic perspective presents the contemporary professional as distressed – because of their own shortcomings, those of their colleagues and/or those of the organisation within which they work.

The therapeutic perspective is the approach we commonly take when thinking about the everyday failures and frustrations of our working days. For example, we may feel unable to cope with myriad requests and think it is because we are insufficiently organised or not competent enough with new technologies. Maybe we feel we are suffering from 'burnout' whereby our initial enthusiasm and commitment have waned into disillusionment and cynicism.

We also often explain away our professional troubles as resulting not from our own inadequacies but from having to work with inadequate fellow professionals. For example, we can feel overburdened because we have to cover for colleagues. This appears to be a common complaint. An Investors in People (2005) survey reported that 80 per cent of staff had colleagues who they thought were 'dead wood' – people who refused to pull their weight: either prioritising their personal life over work or refusing to take on extra responsibility.

In addition to blaming ourselves and our colleagues, we may also feel distressed because of poor practices in the organisations in which we work. For example, research has highlighted factors such as lack of participation in decision-making and poor management style as contributing to high levels of stress among professionals. Huxley *et al.* (2005) undertook a survey of mental health social workers and found that alongside the pressures of workload were complaints of not being valued enough by their managers. Similar results were found in a survey of social workers in Sweden (Tham, 2007). Interviews with social workers suffering from depression (Stanley *et al.*, 2007) point to inadequate support from colleagues and managers as compounding their mental health difficulties.

The identification of 'unhealthy' interpersonal relations at work as the cause of professional distress is highlighted in the mushrooming interest in workplace 'bullying'. Evidence from the UK National Workplace Bullying Advice Line cited by the dedicated resource centre BullyOnLine (www.bullyonline.org) suggests that bullying is rife in professionals' workplaces. Teachers are the largest group of callers to the advice line (accounting for 20 per cent of callers), followed by healthcare employees (12 per cent of callers) and social workers (10 per cent of callers).

Bullying behaviour from managers is seen to contribute to high levels of professional stress. Health and Safety Executive surveys (HSE, 2007) reveal that professionals working in education and health have the highest prevalence rates of work-related stress. Occupations within these fields that were the most stressful were health and social services managers (3.37 per cent) and teaching professionals (2.61 per cent). The National Health Service comes across as an organisation where bullying is commonplace. Half of health visitors, school nurses and community nurses working in the NHS have been bullied by their managers (CPHVA, 2003).

It would appear that bullying behaviour in the workplace is not only prevalent in the professions, but is on the increase. For example, the number of teachers complaining of being bullied by colleagues and managers has increased four-fold in a year, according to the Teacher Support Network (Milne, 2007), which provides a helpline and counselling for teachers. Indeed, a recent survey conducted by the Samaritans (2007) claims that bullying in the workplace affects 80 per cent of employees.

Therapeutic remedies to alleviate distress

If we attribute the distress that professionals experience to their own failings, the shortcomings of their colleagues or their organisation, it makes sense to put in place a range of remedies targeted at these problems.

For example, incompetence with new technologies can be dealt with through ongoing staff development. The difficulties of combining complicated domestic lives with work responsibilities can be addressed through stress counselling. The problem of 'dead wood' can be tackled through rigorous appraisal and performance reviews. In terms of organisational malpractices, there are many self-help resources designed to promote personal well-being in the workplace. Some organisations, such as my own university, have put in place a network of 'dignity advisors'. These individuals are trained to provide advice and guidance to reduce the distress caused by workplace bullying.

While these strategies may provide some beneficial effects for some individuals, it is unlikely that they will significantly alter the work lives of professionals. This is because the way in that the problem is defined takes too narrow a perspective – one that focuses on the individual and their immediate milieu. Clearly, something else is going on that requires a broader overview of the contexts in which professionals work.

The problem of looking only *within* contexts is apparent when one thinks about the huge increase in workplace bullying. The aforementioned BullyOnLine identifies bullying managers in terms of psychological pathologies, such as anti-social personality disorder, narcissistic personality disorder, paranoid personality disorder and borderline personality disorder. Clearly, there may well be individuals suffering from these conditions, but explaining bullying through individual disorders does not really explain the systematic variations between professions or the huge increase in the incidence of bullying.

The inadequacy of taking figures and explanations of workplace bullying at face value is evident if we look at international comparisons. Fevre *et al.* (2008) have analysed data from the European Working Conditions Survey 2005 to construct a 'league table' of bullying. This shows that Finland has the highest incidence of bullying (17.2 per cent) and Bulgaria the least (1.8 per cent). Are we seriously to believe that there is ten times the number of bullies in Finland as in Bulgaria?

It is more probable that the increasing frequency of workplace bullying and its emergence into the language of organisations is nothing more than an increasing awareness that workplace relations can be characterised in this way. As BullyOnLine points out on its webpages: 'Half the population are bullied ... most only realise it when they read this' (www.bullyonline.org).

However, this does not mean that the practices being defined as workplace bullying are fabricated or imagined. It is more likely that the appearance of workplace bullying signals not a brand new phenomenon but a renaming of an old phenomenon. Rather than being an aberration perpetrated by disordered individuals, it can be seen as an inevitable element of occupational life. If this is the case, then no amount of guidance and support will alleviate the distress of the professional. What is needed is a perspective that moves outside the orbit of the organisation for an explanation.

The oppressed professional: a deterministic perspective

The recognition that bullying may be less of an aberration and more of an integral element of occupational life brings a very different perspective to interpreting the troubles and trials of professional life. From this perspective, the professional is no different from any other occupational group.

The position of professionals within contemporary society has long been contested by Marxists. While some align them with the interests of the state and capital, others align them with the working class. However, while the knowledge-basis of their labour may distinguish them from manual workers in one sense, the production, commodification and exploitation of knowledge is in most other ways no different. This is particularly evident in the shift from manufacturing-based economies to knowledge economies.

Professionals, like other workers, receive payment for the creation of surplus value (see Lawn and Ozga, 1988). As such, professionals can never enjoy the supposed autonomy or trust on which their elevated status is supposed to rest. They are, again like other workers, vulnerable to the crises of capital accumulation and legitimation from which all capitalist societies suffer. At times of crisis, professionals, just like other workers, experience intensification of work and deskilling.

Larson (1980), writing over 20 years ago, outlined the processes through which educated labour became proletarianised – drawing attention to the intensification experienced by even such elevated professionals as doctors. Lawn and Ozga (1988) and Apple (1988) have identified similar processes in the working lives of teachers.

Since the late 1980s, professionals have experienced a whole range of further changes which have impacted on their work. At an international level, there are claims that we are in a new era of social history – couched variously in terms of globalisation, postmodernity, post-Fordism and/or the 'information age'. All these aspects have impacted on the lives of professionals in different ways. For example, the growth of post-Fordism has allegedly taken us beyond models of welfare in which 'one size fits all' to one in which professionals are required to offer flexible and personalised services. The 'information age' has allegedly eroded the exclusivity of the knowledge base upon which professionals gain their status – we're all experts now. In the UK, and other nations too, the introduction of quasi-markets into the public sector has allegedly transformed the relationship between professional and client to one of professional and consumer. The rise of new public management and, more recently, the audit culture have brought about new management practices which would have been unrecognisable in the early decades of the post-war welfare state.

While contemporary accounts of the pressures on professionalism may be informed more from post-structuralist rather than from traditional Marxist theories, their representations of professionals as beset by forces outside their control are similar. For example, Shore and Wright (2000: 63) use a Foucauldian analysis to show how higher education professionals have been redefined through the 'audit culture'. 'The audited subject', they argue, 'is recast as a depersonalized unit of economic resource whose productivity and performance must constantly be measured and enhanced'. Similarly, Ball (2001: 211) critiques what he sees as a new mode of social regulation in education 'that bites deeply and immediately into the practice of state professionals – reforming and "re-forming" meaning and identity, producing or making up new professional subjectivities.'

Resisting oppressive practices

Unlike the therapeutic approach, there is no straightforward remedy to relieve the oppressed professional. Because the sources of oppression are located in the wider orbit – not just the national, but the international, orbit – individual professionals can do little or nothing to alleviate their conditions. There may, from a Marxist perspective, be the possibility of change through concerted collective struggle (it is unclear what remedy post-structuralist perspectives offer), but this is difficult for the professional. Indeed, here their supposedly elevated status undermines their capacity for collective and radical resistance.

The tension between upholding professional ethics and resisting through collective action is illustrated by those professional associations that refuse to strike. For example, the Professional Association of Teachers' 'cardinal rule' is that 'Members shall not go on strike in any circumstances' because of 'its negativity and the inevitable damage caused to the interests of those for whom we are responsible'.

In this sense, appeals to professional altruism become a means of social control rather than social advancement. However, while the 'professional as victim' perspective leads to fewer feelings of personal inadequacy, it is both historically and sociologically inaccurate and ultimately serves to deaden, rather than enliven, the professional imagination. It not only underplays the extent to which professionals are powerful (both as individuals and as members of an occupational group), but it also tends to overstate the force of change and indulge in romanticised visions of a 'liberated' professional. The changes which affect professionals are seen to be all-encompassing. The images created are not only of powerlessness but of professionals being overwhelmed. Shore and Wright (2000), for example, speak of 'a wave of change' that has 'swept over' the public sector.

Moreover, any account which casts professionals as victims tends either to over-romanticise earlier epochs of professional autonomy or to hold onto idealised notions of the kind of professionalism that might be achieved without the imposition of state demands. Shore and Wright (2000: 77), again, complain that audit 'encourages the displacement of a system based on autonomy and trust by one based on visibility and coercive accountability'. Ball is similarly concerned that:

> Service commitments no longer have value or meaning and professional judgement is subordinated to the requirements of performativity and marketing... This is part of a larger process of ethical retooling in the public sector which is replacing concern for client need and professional judgement with commercial decision-making. The space for the operation of autonomous ethical codes based on a shared moral language is colonised or closed down.
>
> (2001: 222–3)

These accounts ignore the dark side of the professional. They presume that 'autonomy', 'trust', 'concern for client need' and 'shared moral language' once existed. As many critiques, from the left (e.g. Illich, 1977; Wilding, 1982) as well as the right, have long argued, these properties have always been more imagined than real. At most, they are aspirational. They should certainly never be seen as an accurate empirical description of professional practice.

The imaginative professional: a sociological perspective

I have outlined above two contrasting ways of thinking about the difficulties we face as contemporary professionals. The first approach explains our difficulties through looking at the orbit within which we work – our personal deficiencies, our colleagues' shortcomings and/ or the malpractices of our organisation and its managers. It has no purchase on the broader forces that shape the milieux within which we work. The second approach looks beyond the limits of our private orbits as the cause of our troubles and focuses on those transcending forces – globalisation, postmodernism, post-Fordism, etc. – which constrain our independence and crush our professional commitment. Both approaches are flawed. What is needed is a perspective that encompasses both the immediate orbit and the transcending forces. There can be few more compelling accounts of how such an approach can be developed than the 'sociological imagination' proposed 50 years ago by C. Wright Mills.[1]

The promise of the sociological imagination

The American sociologist C. Wright Mills (1970: 11) uses the term 'sociological imagination' to refer to the capacity to 'understand the larger historical scene in terms of its meaning for the inner life and external career of a variety of individuals'. In order to do this, he argues, it is essential that we distinguish between 'the personal troubles of milieu' and 'the public issues of social structure'.

Troubles, he outlines, 'occur within the character of the individual and within the range of his immediate relations with others ... a trouble is a private matter' (Wright Mills, 1970: 14–15). Issues, on the other hand, 'have to do with matters that transcend these local environments of the individual and the range of his inner life. They have to do with the organization of many such milieux into the institutions of a historical society as a whole ... an issue is a public matter' (Wright Mills, 1970: 15).

In order to illustrate the importance of this distinction, Wright Mills provides a number of examples, including unemployment and divorce. In relation to unemployment, when only one person in a city of 100,000 men is unemployed, it is quite likely that their inability to find work can be explained through their own personal attributes. However, when a significant minority of people are unemployed, it is no longer adequate to account for their lack of work solely in terms of individual failings. Their unemployment is more appropriately explained through reference to the public realm of the labour market and economic structures. The same holds true for marriage. Even though marital breakdown is experienced as an intensely private crisis, the frequency with which it occurs suggests that it is also a public issue. It is, therefore, just as important to look at what is happening in the broader social structure and at the institutions of family and marriage for an explanation of high divorce rates as it is to focus only on the incompatibility of particular couples.

Thus, as people's lives unfold they experience a whole range of difficulties. These difficulties are 'personal' in that they are very real and intensely experienced by the individual in terms of private loss and failure. But they might also need to be understood as more than personal troubles, as public issues that have arisen because of wider changes in society. As Wright Mills argues, 'The individual can understand his own experiences and gauge his own fate *only* by locating himself within his period' (Wright Mills, 1970: 12, my emphasis).

It should hopefully be clear by now that Wright Mills' analytical framework for developing a sociological imagination can usefully be applied to understanding the difficulties that professionals encounter in their daily lives and in their careers. If we go back to our distressed professional, it is clear that if they are the only one in their organisation who is experiencing difficulties, then it would indeed be appropriate to offer them personal support. However, if a significant number of professionals feel that they are stressed or cannot cope, this may point up a public issue.

Take, for instance, older teachers. Research on teacher effectiveness (Day *et al.*, 2006) suggests that new staff teach better. It claims that 80 per cent of teachers in their first seven years 'add value' at or above the expected level, compared to less than 60 per cent of those who had 24 years' experience. Of course, it may well be the case that there are some individuals who actually do become less competent at teaching as they get older. But, surely, it is more probable that teachers who were trained in the 1970s were socialised into a different professional culture. They may 'add value' in ways that are not measured through the current performance indicators. Looked at in this way, the alleged difficulties of older professionals may be viewed as potentially a public issue concerning the transformation of values over what it means to be educated.

If we reflect back to the issues surrounding workplace bullying, there will undoubtedly be psychologically 'disordered' managers in the workplace who systematically demean their staff. However, this is unlikely to provide a compelling explanation for the increasing volume of reported bullying incidents. It is probable that there is a mismatch between the demands of current professional life, with its emphasis on consumer responsiveness and accountability audits, and the experience and expectations of professionals. It may also be that the current emphasis on particular forms of governance and management favours particular kinds of disposition as opposed to others. It is here that we see the linkage between personal and public orbits. Different historical moments both privilege and punish different sensibilities, encourage or discourage the rise of different kinds of men and women.

A sociological imagination facilitates understanding of society in terms of 'its meaning for the inner life and external career of a variety of individuals' (Wright Mills, 1970: 11). The development of a professional imagination will, in parallel, facilitate understanding of the inner life and external career of a variety of professions and professionals. In order to foster this imagination, Wright Mills argues that it is necessary to ask three sorts of question. For our purposes, these questions – borrowed, précised and adapted – address the relational, temporal and dispositional attributes of our profession and our careers.

Relational questions require us to think about the structure of our particular profession as a whole. What are its essential components and how are they related to one another? How does it differ from other varieties of profession? What groups does it include and exclude as it develops?

Temporal questions require us to think about how our profession stands in social history. What trajectory did its professionalisation project take? What groups did it include and exclude in its formation? What are the mechanics by which it is changing? How do its particular features affect, and become affected by, the historical period? What are its essential features at this moment – compared to how it used to be?

Dispositional questions force us to consider what varieties of men and women now prevail in this profession. What varieties are coming to prevail? In what ways are they selected and formed, liberated and repressed, made sensitive and blunted?

Clearly, the answers to these questions will vary according to the profession being considered, but thinking about them enables us to grasp some of the linkage between our own personal troubles and society's public issues. In short, it will help us to become an imaginative professional. Fostering the professional imagination in this way will enable us to move beyond conceptions of ourselves and our work that either overemphasise or underplay individual capacity to effect change.

Conclusion

If professionals are to hold on to their sense of professionalism, they need creative and articulate responses to these changes rather than feelings of hopelessness and/or defensive reaction. The more sophisticated their understandings, the greater the chance of developing such creative and articulate responses.

To quote from Wright Mills (1970: 11–12) one final time, what professionals need:

is a quality of mind that will help them to use information and to develop reason in order to achieve lucid summations of what is going on in the world and what may be happening within themselves ... By such means the personal uneasiness of individuals is focused upon explicit troubles and the indifference of publics is transformed into involvement with public issues.

References

Apple, M.W. (1988) 'Work, class and teaching'. In J. Ozga (ed.), *Schoolwork: Approaches to the Labour Process of Teaching*. Milton Keynes: Open University Press.

Ball, S.J. (2001) 'Performativities and fabrications in the education economy'. In D. Gleeson and C. Husbands (eds), *The Performing School: Managing, Teaching and Learning in a Performance Culture*. London: RoutledgeFalmer.

CPHVA (Community Practitioners' and Health Visitors' Association) (2003) 'Call for ombudsmen to eradicate bullying in the NHS'. Amicus–CPHVA press release, 12 October. Online. <http://www.amicus-cphva.org/default.aspx?page=407> (accessed 17 January 2008).

Day, C., Stobart, G., Sammons, P., Kington, A., Gu, Q., Smees, R. and Mujaba, T. (2006) *Variations in Teachers' Work, Lives and Effectiveness: Final Report for the VITAE Project*. London: Department for Education and Skills.

Fevre, R., Lewis, D., Jones, T. and Robinson, A. (2008) 'Negative behaviour in the British workplace'. Paper given to the American Sociological Association, annual meeting, Boston, August.

Health and Safety Executive (HSE) (2007) *Work-Related Stress: Research and Statistics*. Online. <http://www.hse.gov.uk/stress/research.htm.> (accessed 17 January 2008).

Huxley, P., Evans, S., Gately, C., Webber, M., Mears, A., Pajak, S., Kendall, T., Medina, J. and Katona, C. (2005) 'Stress and pressures in mental health social work: the worker speaks'. *British Journal of Social Work*, 35: 1063–79.

Illich, I. with Zola, I., McKnight, J., Caplan, J. and Shaiken, H. (1977) *Disabling Professionals*. London: Marion Boyars.

Investors in People (2005) *UK Businesses Weighed Down by Deadwood*. Online. <http://www.investorsinpeople.co.uk/Media/PressReleases/Pages/PressReleaseDetail.aspx?PRID=19> (accessed 17 January 2008).

Larson, M. (1980) 'Proletarianization and educated labor'. *Theory and Society*, 9: 89–130.

Lawn, M. and Ozga, J. (1988) 'Work, class and teaching'. In J. Ozga (ed.), *Schoolwork: Approaches to the Labour Process of Teaching*. Milton Keynes: Open University Press.

Millerson, G. (1964) *The Qualifying Associations: A Study in Professionalization*. London: Routledge and Kegan Paul.

Milne, J. (2007) 'Bullying complaints quadruple', *Times Educational Supplement*, 19 October. Online. <http://www.tes.co.uk/search/story/?story_id=2450281> (accessed 17 January 2008).

Samaritans (2007) *Samaritans Stressed out Survey 2007*. Online. <www.samaritans.org> (accessed 17 January 2008).

Shore, C. and Wright, S. (2000) 'Coercive accountability: the rise of audit culture in higher education'. In M. Strathern (ed.), *Audit Cultures: Anthropological Studies in Accountability, Ethics, and the Academy*. London: Routledge.

Siegrist, H. (1994) 'The professions, State and Government in theory and history'. In T. Becher (ed.), *Governments and Professional Education*. Buckingham: Open University Press.

Stanley, N., Manthorpe, J. and White, M. (2007) 'Depression in the profession: social workers' experiences and perceptions'. *British Journal of Social Work*, 37: 281–98.

Tham, P. (2007) 'Why are they leaving? Factors affecting intention to leave among social workers in child welfare'. *British Journal of Social Work*, 37 (7): 1225–46.

Wilding, P. (1982) *Professional Power and Social Welfare*. London: Routledge and Kegan Paul.

Witz, A. (1990) 'Patriarchy and professions: the gendered politics of occupational closure'. *Sociology*, 24.(4): 675–90.

Wright Mills, C. (1970) *The Sociological Imagination*. Harmondsworth: Penguin Books.

Note

[1] *The Sociological Imagination* was originally published by Oxford University Press in 1959.

9 Critical incidents in professional life and learning

Bryan Cunningham

> Experience is a brutal teacher, but you learn fast.
>
> (spoken by the character of C.S. Lewis in the
> play *Shadowlands*, by William Nicholson)

Introduction

This chapter will explore some of the key dimensions of professional learning before turning to what will be my principal focus, a review of the nature of 'critical incidents' and their importance within educational contexts. The critical incident as a dimension of professional life that, while quite often highly stressful – even sometimes traumatic – has the potential to dramatically *accelerate* professional learning, is what makes it worth our attention, I would claim. The whole area of post-qualification professional learning – and indeed learning at work more broadly (Evans, 2002; Rainbird, 2004) – is currently already receiving such attention, but I wish to concern myself here with but one potential component of the process.

My awareness of the power of critical incidents to produce the kind of acceleration referred to above has grown and developed over a number of years, fundamentally assisted by course participants on various programmes, including the EdD (Doctor in Education), who have been willing to share in workshop-style forums the nature of an enormous range of critical incidents. However, it should be strongly emphasised that none of the illustrative material in this chapter will allow the identification of any of the individuals concerned, or their employing organisations, whose confidentiality I have always taken great pains to respect.

The notion of a 'learning professional', as put forward by Guile and Lucas (1999), is one that can usefully underpin such aspects of professionality as a positive approach to continuing professional learning, and professional development. The learning professional is one who seeks out opportunities, within whatever institutional constraints are in place, to *extend* their professional understandings and skills sets, rather than being concerned merely to reflect on those they already possess. In this sense, their attributes will tend to correspond more to those associated with *extended* rather than *restricted* professionalism, the opposition considered to exist by a number of authors (and given an interesting international dimension by Broadfoot *et al.*, 1993) and to be a worthwhile construct in our analysis of professional life and learning.

However, the implicit emphasis of such a commitment to professional learning as is alluded to above is on *formalised* learning; under this heading we might include such activities as attendance at courses, seminars and conferences, participation in organisational systems such as staff review and appraisal, being mentored by a more senior colleague (or, perhaps even a peer) and undertaking accredited programmes offered internally or externally – this being the kind of 'appropriate combination of learning settings' (Eraut, 1994: 13) typically available to individuals. What is not necessarily all that well accommodated by such structured approaches to enhancing professional learning are the kinds of opportunities for *informal,* unplanned, learning that can arise in professional life.

Given that a writer such as Eraut maintains there are 'significant changes in capability or understanding' (Eraut, 1997: 556) to be derived from non-formal learning at work, there does seem to be considerable justification for an examination of what may well constitute, for a number of individuals, an important component of this type of process. The critical incident as one particular manifestation of informal, unplanned or non-formal, learning and as a trigger for change in professional thinking and behaviours is, quite possibly, a major, if extremely infrequently experienced, facet of professional life.

Within education, the notion of critical incidents (not, in fact, that new a coinage, see e.g. Flanagan, 1954) has been gaining currency perhaps more slowly than it has in other professional realms. We have not, for example, adopted the kinds of approach now being seen in the continuing professional development (CPD) of medical practitioners or social workers. In fields such as these, there is now an acknowledgement that critical incidents (though they are more usually termed 'significant events') can play a crucial part in the structured reflection that doctors and social workers are required to engage in – and to document – to provide evidence that they are continuing to learn on the job. As a dimension of CPD in these areas, significant event analysis (SEA) has the especially notable component of unearthing *what went wrong* in certain cases, and it is what can be learnt from this that will inform future practice. The relatively recently introduced procedures for the revalidation of medical practitioners (Deptartment of Health, 1999; 2007) devote considerable attention to articulating why it is that the relevant documents to be compiled by such individuals must incorporate reference to SEA.

Further afield, there is a degree of evidence that in certain ways the notion of critical incidents is being to some extent 'medicalised'. A section of the University of Virginia's website devoted to 'faculty and employee assistance', for example, explains for users that attributes of critical incidents include their being 'acute, stressful and exceed[ing] the normal coping capacities of individuals', and offers information *'to aid recovery'* (University of Virginia, 2006; my emphasis).

Although it might well be argued that education professionals are not so frequently involved in life or death decisions as colleagues in medicine or social work, there are on the other hand clearly ways in which the effectiveness or ineffectiveness of our practice can have very substantial effects on the life *chances* of those whose needs we serve – ultimately, learners in schools, colleges and universities. It is, therefore, a central contention of this chapter that we should not in education overlook the gains in our professional understandings that may accrue from analysing critical incidents we experience.

Defining 'critical incident'

In the normal course of a busy, sometimes harassed or even beleaguered, professional life it is evident that very numerous interactions and events take place, day in, day out. These will usually include conversations, dialogue with others in the context of teaching or training events, confrontations of varying degrees of seriousness, the receipt of one form or other of directive or guidance note, etc. Many of these interactions and events are thus quite likely to be *undramatic* ones – to an observer, they may even appear wholly banal or trivial. No specific event is *inherently* critical; its criticality exists only in its perception as such by the individual experiencing it, and contextualising it.

At certain times, interaction will be with individuals or organisations beyond our immediate professional sphere; a government circular, for example, may require if not an immediate response then perhaps fairly speedy implementation of an initiative. Of these very many 'happenings', what is it that causes some to stand out – to embody a *criticality*?

> Incidents happen, but critical incidents are produced by the way we look at a situation: a critical incident is an *interpretation* of the significance of an event. To take something as a critical incident is a value judgement we make, and the basis of that judgement is the significance we attach to the *meaning* of the incident.
>
> (Tripp, 1993: 8; emphasis added)

To explore this notion, and before offering my own working definition of critical incident, I would propose that one or more of the following criteria will apply – they may well not appear to do so instantaneously, but will be experienced as a result of a period of reflection.

The first, and for me most valuable, construct in the analysis of what renders critical an event in professional life is its propensity to create a disturbance in our professional *equilibrium*. We are in one regard or another 'unbalanced' by what has taken place – a critical incident may be experienced emotionally in a roughly similar way to that in which the sudden braking of a bus or train affects the standing passenger physically. This notion of one's equilibrium being disturbed is an important one, and is illustrated by Tripp in a number of interesting ways in his key text on critical incidents in teaching, fairly essential reading for anyone wishing to delve more deeply into the notion than this chapter is able to. Seeking for an underlying reason why a specific event may be viewed as critical, a general theme could probably be said to be that nothing in one's prior training or professional experience has offered adequate preparation for it and this is why we are unsettled. To pursue a little further the analogy with the physical effects of a sudden braking, what causes the discomfort – or actual injury, of course, on occasion – is that none of our prior 'passenger experiences' were able to teach us how to effectively brace ourselves in a situation where no warning that it would be sensible to do so has been given.

This unpreparedness may possibly offer an overarching explanation for why some, infrequently experienced, events possess the criticality that many simply do not. However, it does not necessarily provide any insight into actual causation, the important area to which I will shortly turn my attention.

With all of the foregoing in mind, I would propose the following as a working definition of 'critical incident' in professional life:

> A critical incident comprises an event in professional life that creates a significant disturbance of our understanding of important principles or of effective practice, and which following a period of focused reflection will be experienced as a turning point.

For some readers, in introducing the notion of 'turning point' I may possibly seem to be guilty of overdramatising matters. However, as I indicated near the start of the chapter, my engagement with critical incidents is by no means based purely on subjective conclusions arrived at by reference to significant events in my own professional life history. The kinds of 'recurring themes' and (highly disguised) specific events alluded to below, which it is hoped will convincingly convey a sense of criticality, are all ones derived from, and collated following, considerable experience working with often highly successful professionals in education; I would argue such terms as 'turning point' – or 'disturbance' – in no way overstate the kinds of impact, and changes consequent on critical incidents, that such individuals' professional biographies have included.

However, before attempting to review a range of possible causative events that may, over time, be definable as critical incidents, I would wish (besides acknowledging the fact that in no way will I be drawing on any data gathered by empirically sound means; my review is not a data-laden one in the way that, for instance, David Tripp's work, cited above, is; only one passage, in a later section, approximates to a summarised case study) to include here three relatively extended *preliminaries* which in my view are essential for a full understanding of 'criticality'.

First, it would appear to be the case – to perhaps risk stating the obvious – that an event that for *one* individual is a critical incident may well constitute, for *another,* nothing of the kind. It may be, for example, that the first individual may experience the event as critical because at the precise moment it occurred they were already experiencing a particularly susceptible emotional state. Significant events in our professional lives do on occasion have an unfortunate propensity to be coincident with major upheavals in the realm of the personal. When this happens it might well be the case that an event that ordinarily we might be able to confront with a degree of calm confidence possesses a far more disturbing, daunting character. The phrase 'the straw that broke the camel's back' may possibly come to many readers' minds in this sort of context.

Second, I have included above in my definition the proposition that 'criticality' as a dimension of an event often emerges not instantaneously but 'following a period of focused reflection'. The reflection may be a wholly individual, insular, process, or it may be taking place as a dimension of formal or informal professional talk; in the former case, we could invoke the likelihood of the event featuring in a dialogue between mentor and mentee (where the person who has experienced the event in question happens to be in such a workplace relationship) for instance. A skilled mentor will be able to bring out, and insightfully review, the professional ramifications of what has been described by their mentee as having taken place; this elucidation may be a highly important part of the process of conceptualising an event as a critical incident.

Mentoring dialogues, and various other forms of professional talk, are not usually, of course, 'one-offs'. They are typically part of an ongoing interactive process. Wholly unsupported/unstructured, individual, reflection on an event that has been in one way or another

settling is also generally something that takes place over a period
time. These are important considerations to bear in mind for
anyone subscribing to the somewhat beguiling notion of the critical
incident as being a revelation – a 'lightbulb moment'.

This particular descriptor of critical incidents is one encountered
not infrequently in discussion with fellow professionals, but it is
probably not all that helpful. Unless, that is, we put to one side our,
up till now, most typical visualisation of what happens when we
switch on a light. For the present, at least, we almost certainly tend
to think in terms of the immediate bringing of light into darkness
that we obtain with a traditional (but, incidentally, perhaps
imminently to be banned) tungsten filament bulb. However, I would
promote an awareness, for comparative purposes, of what happens
when one of the newer, energy-efficient, bulbs receives electrical
current when switched on: what takes place is a *gradual*, full
illumination of a space, following a period during which the glow
from this kind of light source – at least until available technology
improves – is relatively dim. So, if we do wish to endow the concept
of a 'lightbulb moment' with any validity in the specific context of
critical incidents, it is probably through engaging with the above
comparison that we can legitimately do so.

Third, it may also be illusory to conceive of the critical incident
itself as being exclusively a single isolated event – such things as an
'out of the blue' classroom confrontation, for example. I would
contend that the notion of critical incident is most profitably viewed
as being a more flexible one, able to accommodate a *series* of events,
connected in ways that are chronological, structural or emotional –
or an amalgam of these.

Furthermore, on occasion there may perhaps have been what we
could refer to as one or more precursors of a critical incident under
study. An 'atmosphere', a sense of expectancy or of imminent change
in a professional organisation, for instance, would not in themselves

necessarily invalidate such constructs as 'unpreparedness' for an event. In certain ways, the kind of foreboding alluded to here may, over time, even be seen as a dimension of the actual incident itself. An example might perhaps be the appointment of a new senior manager, whose arrival in an organisation has been preceded by a degree of anxiety (say, based on what has been gleaned of their recent professional history) that they will wish to introduce certain radical, potentially worrying, changes. If such changes then do materialise, and they possess for one or more individuals a criticality, it seems quite artificial to separate them out in any analysis from the appointment that preceded them, and the sense of anxiety that this generated.

Series of events (taking place with or without any forewarning) could include such things as:

- a set of classroom exchanges with a learner over successive sessions that *builds to* an actual confrontation

- a period of correspondence with a superior that *in total*, e.g. after three or four 'instalments' (memos, emails), is seen to represent a challenge

- a structured observation of one's teaching or training practice, followed by a debriefing, which in turn is followed by the writing of a 'self-evaluation' statement (the *whole process* taking, say, a week or so)

- a particularly 'difficult' mentoring or appraisal meeting with a subordinate, with the individual concerned continuing to press certain points at intervals, and using various media, for a period afterwards.

Some recurrent themes in the nature of critical incidents

The first dimension of critical incidents that recurs in a number of narratives describing them is their apparent *trivialness* when first experienced. However, over time they have begun to assume greater and greater salience for someone. The overheard, offhand remark, for example, in which some aspect of one's character or behaviour has been referred to, or an exchange of the utmost brevity with a student in a group, might fall under the heading, when first considered, of 'trivial'. However, as Tripp usefully points out, the very fact that an individual *recalls* what took place, and chooses to recount it, is in itself an indicator of the event's possible criticality. (Tripp, 1993: 35).

On balance, however, it is probably true that the dimensions of many critical incidents were *never* in any subjective, or often objective, sense trivial to the individuals experiencing them. Some of the significant *elements* of criticality – identified either in isolation or, occasionally, in combination – that have emerged for me in my facilitation practice over a period of years have included:

- a degree of conflict or confrontation (e.g. with peers, managers or learners in the case of teachers/lecturers)

- the impact(s) of major organisational change (e.g. restructuring, relocation, budgetary cuts – 'organisational stress')

- new, externally set, requirements applicable to employees (e.g. the introduction of tighter monitoring of performance, compulsory CPD)

- failure to achieve a specific professional goal such as a promotion

- the – often unsought-after – acquisition of new responsibilities such as a line management role, or a far broader remit than previously held.

- situations that are the opposite of the previous one, i.e. where actual or *de facto* demotions have affected someone

- professional dilemmas, anxiety about which caused a high degree of personal stress (how to respond to a challenging situation, for example, or far more positively, whether to accept a post with greater responsibilities – but likely to hold more daunting challenges as well)

- receipt, in one form or another, of a directive that in one or more respect appears to require an individual to follow a course of action that is incongruent with their conception of what is appropriate professional behaviour; it may pose a dilemma of a specifically *ethical* type

- immediate emotional reactions stemming from events, including certain of the above, that summon up such descriptions as 'undermined', 'devalued', 'challenged', 'humiliated' or, simply, 'hurt'.

Then, to turn more to the kinds of 'outcomes' that appear to have been 'thematically' represented, these as I have encountered them have quite often included such phenomena as:

- a period during which the degree of negative emotional sentiment, or 'ego damage', experienced was severe enough to effectively preclude any short-term positive and effective action on the part of the affected individual

- a drastic reorientation of professional practice, priorities or both of these

- 'downshifting' within a profession – often to seek the calmer waters of a less responsible position

- its opposite, viz. a – perhaps quite unexpected – elevation to a position carrying significant additional responsibilities

- actual 'flight' from a profession, entailing either a career change or a period – where financially feasible – of further study[1] (offering the opportunity, sometimes, for structured reflection on developments within a professional sector, possibly even that an individual has just left)

- crucially important new professional learning that has laid a foundation for change, or endowed someone with the confidence to seek progression within or beyond the employing organisation.

From both of the above sets of illustrations, it will be clear that while many of the specific elements and outcomes have strikingly negative connotations, not all of them do. This seems to raise some interesting issues, and it is to these issues – of negativity and positivity – that I will thus now turn.

The 'negative vs positive' question

Quite possibly the most frequently posed question relating to critical incidents when introducing the idea to a group is 'must they always have negative connotations?', or variants on this form of words. The answer would appear to be that while the causes of critical incidents are, on balance, often far more centred on negative, concerning, or actually disturbing, events than on positive ones, their outcomes may equally often be, especially in the longer term and viewed *as part of a process of formative learning*, positive. And a certain, particularly broad, conception of the critical incident would encompass such positive events as gaining, unexpectedly, a long-desired promotion or receiving a degree of praise for one's performance in the workplace hitherto totally absent. (In these kinds of eventualities, th 'disturbance of equilibrium' we have explored probably arises because an endemic sense of low self-esteem and failure to achieve is dramatically altered).

Extreme manifestations of highly negative critical incidents are represented by such life-changing occurrences as redundancy. Where this afflicts an individual for whom it has been a completely unimaginable possibility – their self-perception having been that they were so highly valued in an organisation that they would be indispensable and therefore invulnerable – then a situation of almost total disorientation may result. A package of sentiments extending from anxiety through anger, betrayal and even grief may be experienced. The immediate shock of redundancy may well indeed be one of life's major blows.

Yet we seem to encounter from time to time individuals for whom the *ultimate* outcome of even such a profoundly unsettling event as redundancy has been a highly positive one. Surveying one's options after losing what, certainly for most education professionals, has been the central occupation in one's life can reveal potential areas of endeavour (finances allowing) as retraining, going into business, or a return to studying. I am confident that I am far from alone in having encountered during a career in education individuals who have followed these kinds of paths 'post-redundancy', and who are able to speak of the aftermath of what was often a very painful event as having been, in fact, life-enhancing. Resourcefulness, even courageousness, has come to the fore as such individuals have confronted the necessity of reconstructing a life with professional meaning.

To write of such things is, of course, to focus on what lies at the extreme ends of a continuum of professional highs and lows, admittedly. Less shocking events than redundancy may similarly have *immediate* dimensions that are overwhelmingly negative but also a ɔnger-term criticality that derives from new opportunities having opened up. An academic relinquishing a managerial role such as head of department because its responsibilities had begun to induce stress-related illnesses will perhaps experience the act of 'stepping down' as something inadequate, or defeatist; therefore it may be felt as a kind of disempowerment. And yet, once new 'lower status' circumstances have been adjusted to, there can open up for such an individual vastly expanded amounts of time for the research and scholarship that they probably came into university teaching in the first place to devote themselves to.

Effective professional learning from critical incidents

If certain of the limitations of the 'reflective practitioner' model have been highlighted by Guile and Lucas (1999), they include the fact that it does not necessarily require that reflection be turned into action. To rather oversimplify the case, it is that reflection may become mere 'navel-gazing' rather than a dimension of professional life that leads to change and improvement. We may deepen our understanding of our performance – its limitations and deficiencies in particular – but whether adopting developmental strategies for moving forward is going to happen is unclear.

In this vein, having stressed the value of professional dialogue – talk – in examining the values and practices that have been thrown into prominence by a particular critical incident, we should also review some ways in which such talk might eventually translate into change. As a character in one of Richard Yates' novels expressed this (when commenting on the implausibility of the plot line of a short story written by a co-student in a creative writing class): 'And even then – even then I'm not sure if talk alone is gonna do the job. I'm not sure if anybody's life ever got turned around by talk alone. Seems to me we need some kind of a thing in there too' (Yates, 2005: 190).

What might in fact be the nature of the 'thing' that we cou
envisage as being crucial to the process of facilitating any meaningfu
'follow-up' to reflection on, and discursive exploration of, a critical
incident? One possible, structural, element of such follow-up may be
located in the context of an organisation's review and appraisal
mechanisms. Typically these incorporate guided questioning around
areas such as:

- the past year's achievements

- difficulties encountered and how these were, or are being,
  resolved

- whether there are any perceived obstacles to an individual
  performing optimally

- what supporting strategies a manager might usefully deploy
  with regard to the preceding point.

In a forum where these are not only legitimate strands of a discussion
but are also required as part of an organisation's human resources
strategy, we have, it seems, fairly clear opportunities for appraisees
to weave into proceedings any critical incidents they have experienced
since the last review/appraisal 'cycle'. They may not do so formally,
i.e. by prefacing their narrative by designating particular events as
'critical', but they can bring them to the appraiser's attention under
the kinds of headings set out above. Stemming from this, practical
outcomes could well be conceivable: the 'thing' may consist, for
instance, of an undertaking by an appraiser to advocate or negotiate
on behalf of their appraisee with a view to bringing about a situation
where they are, say, given greater responsibility or autonomy, or
greater access to administrative support.

Possibly an even more formal and structured – some might even
add the word 'disciplined' – forum that could be profitably exploited

pursue the implications and potential outcomes of a critical incident is the action learning set. The workings of these, and their value within professional education, are particularly well reviewed by McGill and Beaty (2001). From my own past membership of such a 'set', it was notable how in reality a proportion of the issues, questions or concerns being presented by set members essentially had their genesis in recently experienced significant events in their professional lives. Where one has the luxury of the time necessary for full and effective participation in an action learning set, it can quite probably be an unparalleled opportunity to take forward discussion of a critical incident; indeed, the use of the word *'action'* in the designation of such a forum says a great deal about their characteristics when operating optimally for participants.

And there are other conceivable practical outcomes of professional talk – of any kind – with critical incidents at their heart. I have an especially vivid recollection of a situation that arose in a particular further education (FE) college where I was teaching, when I was a 'witness', as a bystander, to the aftermath of a critical incident – and to the unfolding over a period of time of certain wholly practical outcomes. A colleague had experienced an especially stressful teaching session with what was described as being an extremely demotivated group, largely mismatched to the 'pre-vocational' course that they were following. A fairly public staffroom discussion was taking place – comprising a highly visible wetting of shoulders – with, at its core, a very prominent question: 'Why aren't we offering these students something that *does* suit their needs?' For the colleague principally concerned, a terrible (their word) teaching session had brought to a head this simmering question, and in this sense had indeed been an event possessing a criticality.

What then happened was that another colleague, a highly experienced and greatly respected teacher, with strong presence and interpersonal skills, intervened in the discussion to offer his own view.

He concurred that a significant change in the curricular offer t
certain learner groups should indeed be set in motion. He offered
immediate collaborative assistance in the writing of a new course
proposal document, and his advocacy – as a relatively senior teacher
in the college – in taking certain ideas forward. Both of these things
did actually then happen; to the clear benefit of both teachers such
as the first colleague mentioned here, and to the learner groups
concerned, a significantly refined 'pre-vocational' pathway was
introduced into the college's offer in what was quite a surprisingly
speedy and smooth fashion. There were 'turning points' for teachers,
learners and an organisation, all deriving from what had happened
in one classroom and then been subsequently discussed within a
small staffroom. (An interesting manifestation, incidentally, of the
kinds of *participation* – engagement in actions and interactions – in a
community of practice that Wenger (1998) persuasively drew
attention to.)

Constraints and other issues

Of course, the narrative above (though absolutely honest) may strike
many readers as somewhat far-fetched in modern circumstances. The
action consequent on the critical incident was in an important sense
the result of the intervention of an individual with some *gravitas*,
and whose position within a hierarchy endowed them with more
potential than might otherwise have been the case to 'take things
forward'. Relatively small FE colleges during the period in question
– the very early 1980s – had a degree of autonomy in how they were
able to respond to local needs, and switch resourcing, that is probably
quite hard to envisage now. This is not the same as saying that it
would in present times be totally unfeasible that the events described
could take place; a version of them is not, for me, completely out of
the question, although constraints of funding, audit and quality

ssurance would probably entail a far longer time lag between the stimulus for change – the staffroom discussion – and the realisation of the change itself.

It is, then, only appropriate to turn now, briefly, to the kinds of factors that may operate as constraints to 'turning points', whether these be at the level of the individual or an organisation. Certainly the idea of 'constraints' does seem to be applicable at both the personal/professional level and at that of the organisation – where this term encompasses such entities as faculties, departments, etc. as well as such 'whole' organisations as schools, colleges, universities or educational administrative areas.

With regard to the personal/professional level, the learning deriving from a critical incident may not always allow for consequent *action*. An individual's new self-realisation, following a critical incident, that they 'need to move on' will only be built on where the practical dimensions of their situation, as well as the emotional ones, are conducive to this. We may thus conceive of situations where a new understanding or an 'emotional intelligence' (Goleman, 1999) appears to point someone in a particular direction but they are unable to follow this for one or more reasons. For example, a specific incident (or linked series of events, in a certain case that comes to my mind) strongly signals that for a full-time lecturer the most sensible course of action is now to seek, within their employing organisation, a change in status to a fractional appointment. This, the individual judges, is a transition that can allow them to continue to cope with the demands of a teaching career (which they emphatically do not wish to abandon altogether). The person is an expert practitioner, with student evaluations of their classroom, and tutorial, work over the years having been consistently highly positive. To continue to operate as a teacher and maintain such commendable standards of practice, they believe that they will simply need to arrange to have fewer teaching commitments in the organisation. However, the employer holds to the position that part-time staff have no significant role to play in this particular institution, and essentially requires that either the existing arrangement continues, or the lecturer resigns their post.[2] This is what the individual concerned, with significant regret (and not a little anger), ultimately feels forced to do.

Similarly 'take it or leave it' attitudes and/or policies have also been of high relevance in a number of other narratives shared with me by individuals whose scope for action – whatever the professional learning from a critical incident would appear to dictate – has been severely curtailed by practical considerations. One further example of such a syndrome is very briefly outlined below.

This narrative revolved around the grading of teaching competence, as observed and judged by trainers on a 'licence to practise' programme of initial teacher education (ITE). In a UK context, ITE is very tightly monitored by bodies such as the Office for Standards in Education (Ofsted), the Teacher Development Agency (TDA) and Standards Verification UK (SVUK). One aspect of such monitoring is that classroom performance during both ITE programmes and, subsequently, 'on the job' (either as part of schools and colleges' internal review processes or as a facet of external inspection) is required to be graded against a numerical scale, although this has not always been the case; in the case of the college sector, for instance, the grading of classroom teaching began in 1993.

One particular individual, a teacher trainer, experienced the introduction of grading for trainees *on ITE programmes* as a wholly negative innovation. From their perspective, grading may well have had a utility as a management tool, for use by employers or inspectors, perhaps especially where underperformance appeared to be evident; grades, and their associated descriptors, could be relevant in explaining to teachers exactly in which domains of practice it was being held that their teaching was deficient.

However, at the vital *initial* training stage probably outweighing any ostensible benefits attached to grading would be the risks of either engendering a damaging complacency in those trainees being judged 'Grade 1' teachers, or, worse, severely denting the self-esteem of a trainee being awarded a low grade, and badly demotivating them.[3] Yet, in a situation where national guidelines made it virtually impossible for any individual trainer to evade implementing a grading system, how were they to come to terms with this when it ran so significantly in opposition to their conception of the nature of an effective, supportive (and nurturing, even) training programme? The autonomy held to be such a crucial dimension of professional life (Olssen *et al.*, 2004) – the ability to act with discretion (Freidson, 2001) – was simply removed, by diktat. As with the previous example, the sense of powerlessness (an *actual* powerlessness, in fact) relatively speedily led the individual concerned to switch direction away from what had been a long-standing involvement in ITE, rather than compromise certain principles held dear to them. It was quite clearly the case that their *preferred* course of action would have been to remain engaged with ITE, but opt out of having to award grades to trainees in respect of the all-important process of assessing practical teaching. However, certain realities dictated that an 'exogenously generated, rule-following [procedure]' brought about a wholly unacceptable situation in which their professionalism was self-perceived as having been render[ed] into a form of performance, that what count[ed] as professional practice rest[ed] upon meeting fixed, externally imposed judgements' (Ball, 2004: 4).

We might, of course, conjecture that a 'middle way' could have been a possible course of action for the individual concerned. They could have chosen to remain in a field of practice they valued, and saw as highly worthy, adopting a kind of 'camouflage'; they had, it seems, available to them the possible strategy of actually awarding the grades required, while at the same time making absolutely

explicit to trainees the fact that they did not support the policy, ar.
supportively offering them the perspective that teaching performance
overall was something they viewed as infinitely too complex to
capture its quality numerically. Had they taken this third, somewhat
subversive, approach to their professional dilemma, then such
constructs as 'strategic compliance' (Shain and Gleeson, 1999: 456) or
'cynical compliance' (Ball, 2003: 222) can be seen as probably being
appropriate to the case.

The foregoing two illustrations of the operation of 'constraints to
action' represent but a very small sampling of the scenarios brought
to the kinds of events now to be briefly described.

The nature, purpose and management of critical incident workshops

An especially rich source of my own professional learning connected
with critical incidents has lain in a relatively long-term involvement,
as facilitator, of 'workshop' style events. It would be wholly
inappropriate explicitly to make mention of specific critical incidents
brought for discussion to any of these: as I indicate below, one of the
prime necessities for their effectiveness is that participants are
absolutely guaranteed strict confidentiality. Nevertheless, for readers
who may themselves, either now or at some stage in the future, find
themselves similarly involved, this section of the chapter offers some
rationale, and guidelines, for the activity. It cannot, however, aim at
the kinds of comprehensive treatment of issues as might be contained
in a manual.

A critical incident workshop ('forum' might equally well be adopted
as a description) ought to have as its underpinnings certain *core
principles*:

- Attendance is understood to be *entirely optional*.

- The issue of *confidentiality of proceedings* is given special prominence – colleagues of mine have often used the construct of 'Chatham House rules' as a device here, although in international contexts it would probably have considerably less meaning.

- The *ethos* of the events is, above all, articulated and agreed as a collegial, supportive, one. (To illustrate how this might be manifested, workshop facilitators could cite the absolute inappropriateness of criticising, or appearing to criticise, a workshop member's response, as they have described it, to particular events.)

- The *objectives* of a workshop need to be broadly viewed as (1) allowing participants to engage with even more fully – through the process of explaining it to others – the nature and outcomes of a critical incident they have experienced, and (2) identifying any linking themes that may emerge from a review of the incidents brought to, and shared at, the event.

- The *facilitator's* role, in accordance with general principles in effective facilitation, is very much built on skills such as active listening, confident but unobtrusive timekeeping, and monitoring the focus and cohesion of the group.

In terms of *cautions*, the following might be found to be of value:

- The *size* of a workshop group tends to become rather unwieldy once more than six or seven participants are taking part and wishing to describe, and hear any responses to, 'their' incidents: the time needed meaningfully to review, say, ten critical incidents can add up to an exhausting event, given the intensity of discussion and emotion typically generated; the basic issue or attention spans is also highly pertinent here.

- In terms of the *physical environment*, cramped or – possibly even worse – overly large spaces are rarely conducive to comfortable discussion. The potential hazards from extraneous noise or actual interruptions should also always be considered when judging the suitability of a physical space for a critical incident workshop.

- The issue of *boundaries* – drawing to some extent from good practice in counselling – has to be out in the open: the purpose of the workshop cannot lay in the domain of problem-solving, and in as positive and supportive a manner as possible this ought to be communicated to participants.

- A facilitator should be highly aware of the propensity of critical incident workshops to generate, on occasions, tension or even actual distress in individual participants, and should be prepared to assume a more prominent role at any such points to calm a situation.

In *very general terms* (no two critical incident workshops are ever replicas the one of the other), the actual proceedings within a workshop group over, say, a two- or three-hour period, with necessary breaks, might follow the sort of pattern I shall attempt to outline below.

The facilitator welcomes the group (of no larger size than six to eight members, ideally), provides (or revisits) the *rationale* for the workshop, and briefly outlines its anticipated *outcomes*; issues such as the possible identification of common themes arising from participants' critical incidents, the establishment of an ongoing support network, etc. are the types of specifics that are typically referred to. Important practicalities relating to timekeeping, eschewing interrupting speakers, turn-taking and the all-important matter of confidentiality are also woven into the introduction – the scene-setting.

In turn, workshop participants are then invited to contribute:

- a succinct review of the context and nature of the incident itself – e.g. its timing, and the principal actors and 'ingredients'

- the process that led to its being perceived as critical – what type of reflection took place? Individual? Discussion with one other person? Discussion within a group?

- the most significant elements in the ensuing professional learning that took place

- the actions/developments that were consequent on this learning, or which are still in process.

Between each member's contribution, proceedings can very usefully be 'punctuated' by segments in which other participants can, in a managed way – the facilitator acting as 'chair' at these points – take the opportunity to express their empathy, or actual solidarity, and to raise any questions that they may have been left with from the exposition. Sometimes, listeners may well also signpost the fact that, in some regards, certain dimensions of a narrative are ones that they too will be touching on in their own.

By the end of the above process, a skilled facilitator having mentally noted any important recurring themes, or points of very special interest, will ask the group whether they themselves had been aware of links or commonalities. (Two points of guidance may be valuable here: first, that making mental notes, as referred to above, seems infinitely preferable in an environment where confidentiality has been emphasised – we are pre-empting individuals wondering 'why is the facilitator writing down some of the things we are saying?';

second, it detracts somewhat from a group's sense of ownership of the events they have experienced if the facilitator uses his or her position to summarise *what for him/her* was most revealing in the narratives.)

The concluding segment of an effectively managed critical incidents workshop should be both brief and reiterative of the considerations relating to confidentiality. It can also valuably indicate to the group the possibility, at least, *of participation in the workshop itself* as, on yet further reflection on the incidents that have been shared, coming to be viewed as one of the ways in which understanding of these incidents may have been deepened.

Some conclusions

I have endeavoured in this chapter to approach the concept of 'critical incident' from a perspective that views professional learning as a multifaceted process accommodating both formal and 'accidental' learning. I have aimed to allow the reader to envisage the very wide range of significant events that may, over time, emerge as possessing a 'criticality'. My other principal tasks have revolved around exploring the *value* of critical incidents, and exemplifying their potential for bringing about positive changes in spite of their frequently unsettling, even distressing, primary nature. Essentially, I believe that the processes of reviewing and deconstructing critical incidents encountered in their working lives offer professionals in education very significant increments to the quality of their understandings.

These understandings do not, of course, accrue only to individuals on the basis of whether they have experienced critical incidents. Further, although I have drawn attention to the notion of an *acceleration* of professional learning deriving from critical incidents, we should remind ourselves of the kinds of larger dimensions of reflective practice that Moore describes in an excellent exploration of constructs and discourses around 'the good teacher':[4]

> whereas some forms of reflection tend to focus on the immediate, to be self-referential, and to feed directly into plans, tactics and strategies (an essentially instrumentalist orientation), reflexivity focuses more on the broader picture... and hence is part of a 'slower', longer-term route to improved practice through developing self-understandings that may feed into teaching in ways that are often not planned in advance.
>
> (Moore, 2004:151)

It may prove to be the case, however, that, in what Barnett has termed elsewhere in this volume times of 'supercomplexity' for professionals, the critical incident takes on even greater significance within the overall nature of reflection. If we are indeed witnessing a growth in the number and variety of professional transactions and the emergence of such facets of this growth as 'multiple discourses' (Barnett, 2000), then we might logically conjecture that from out of all this burgeoning interaction a greater number of individual exchanges/conflicts than ever previously will contain the seeds of criticality.

A further piece of seemingly plausible horizon-gazing is prompted by another notion introduced in this volume, by Power: that of the relationship between *private troubles* and *public issues* (Wright Mills, 1970). If these are indeed uncertain, supercomplex, times, then quite possibly we may find that an even more pressured educational environment will be one in which an even larger number of events become critical. Many policy, and societal, trends presently impacting on educational professionals are from some angles militating against the calm and self-confidence of such workers. The growth in target-setting, audit cultures, learner entitlements, 'cost-recovery' and for-profit ventures, along with continuing public questioning of standards of probity and performance in education, will all probably tend to increase the susceptibility that I alluded to earlier on. In other words, disequilibrium in the wider world, as developed societies adjust to such phenomena as diminishing resources and more-or-less permanent challenges to their security, as well as to forces more to do with lack of respect for authority and so on, has seemingly strong potential to exacerbate disequilibrium at the scale of the professional workplace.

The individual experiencing a major, potentially life-changing, event within his or her educational institution is, if my tentative argument here is accepted as a valid one, yoked in any number of not necessarily immediately evident ways to changes taking place outside that institution – perhaps even changes being witnessed on a global scale. Such a contention might well be proven to be a somewhat grandiose one, inflating the significance of critical incidents well beyond what is credible and convincing. Even if this is so, the attributes of the events as I have outlined them in this chapter, and the contributions they make to broadening and deepening our professional learning, already sufficiently merit our attention, I would claim.

References

Ball, S. (2003) 'The teacher's soul and the terrors of performativity'. *Journal of Education Policy*, 18 (2): 215–28.

Ball, S. (2004) 'Education reform as social barberism: Economism and the end of authenticity'. Lecture to Scottish Educational Research Association Annual Conference, 25–27 November, Perth.

Broadfoot, P. and Osborn, M. with Gilly, M. and Bucher, A. (1993) 'The meaning of professionalism'. In *Perceptions of Teaching: Primary School Teachers in England and France*. London: Cassell.

Department of Health (1999) *Supporting Doctors, Protecting Patients: A Consultation Paper*. London: Department of Health, Publications and Statistics.

Department of Health (2007) *Trust, Assurance and Safety: The Regulation of Health Professionals*. White Paper, Cm 7013. London: The Stationery Office.

Eraut, M. (1994) *Developing Professional Knowledge and Competence*. London: Falmer Press.

Eraut, M. (1997) 'Perspectives on defining "the Learning Society" '. *Journal of Education Policy*, 12 (6): 551–8.

Evans, K.M. (2002) *Working to Learn: Transforming Learning in The Workplace*. London: Kogan Page.

Flanagan, J.C. (1954) 'The critical incident technique'. *Psychological Bulletin*, 51 (4): 327–58.

Freidson, E. (2001) *Professionalism: The Third Logic*. Cambridge: Polity Press.

Goleman, D. (1999) *Working with Emotional Intelligence*. London: Bloomsbury.

Guile, D. and Lucas, N. (1999) 'Rethinking initial teacher education and professional development in further education: towards the learning professional'. In A. Green and N. Lucas (eds.), *FE and Lifelong Learning: Realigning The Sector for the Twenty-First Century*. Bedford Way Papers. London: Institute of Education.

Kolb, D.A. (1984) *Experiential Learning: Experience as the Source of Learning and Development*. London: Prentice-Hall.

McGill, I. and Beaty, L. (2001) *Action Learning: A Guide for Professional, Management and Educational Development*. London: Kogan Page.

Moore, A. (2004) *The Good Teacher: Dominant Discourses in Teaching and Teacher Education*. London: RoutledgeFalmer.

Nicholson, W. (1990) *Shadowlands*. Harmondsworth: Penguin.

Olssen, M., Codd, J. and O'Neill, A-M. (2004) 'Markets, professionalism, trust'. In M. Olssen *et al.*, *Education Policy: Globalisation, Citizenship and Democracy*. London: Sage.

Rainbird, H. (2004) *Workplace Learning in Context*. London: Routledge.

Shain, F. and Gleeson, D. (1999) 'Under new management: changing conceptions of teacher professionalism and policy in the further education sector'. *Journal of Education Policy*, 14 (4): 445–62.

Tripp, D. (1993) *Critical Incidents in Teaching: Developing Professional Judgement*. London: Routledge.

University of Virginia (2006) Faculty and Employee Assistance Program. Online. <http://www.healthsystem.virginia.edu/internet/feap/critical-incidents.cfm> (accessed 22 November 2007).

Wenger, E. (1998) *Communities of Practice: Learning, Meaning and Identity*. Cambridge: Cambridge University Press.

Wright Mills, C. (1970) *The Sociological Imagination*. Harmondsworth: Penguin.

Yates, R. (2005) *Young Hearts Crying*. London: Methuen. (Originally published by Delacorte Press/Seymour Lawrence, US.)

Notes

[1]   A number of Doctor in Education enrolments have been cited by the individuals themselves as having come about because of this kind of situation.

[2]   The upshot was the latter option being taken by the individual concerned; however, employment legislation has subsequently been amended in such a way as would now notably strengthen the lecturer's case.

[3]   Ofsted uses the following scale for inspection purposes: Grade 1 Outstanding; Grade 2 Good; Grade 3 Satisfactory; Grade 4 Inadequate.

[4]   It appears entirely plausible that in other professional domains besides teaching the processes alluded to by Moore might be identified.

10 Critical professionalism in an age of supercomplexity
Ronald Barnett

Introduction

In a 'liquid' age (as we have learnt to understand it from Zygman Bauman (2000)), being a professional is fraught with difficulty. A particular difficulty that I want to explore in this chapter turns on the notion of 'professing' that lies within the terms 'profession' and 'professional'. Just what is it to 'profess' in the modern age? For, in this age, the claims to authority that formed the basis of the professional's legitimacy as a professional are continually challenged. The ice cracks within professional life. Against these considerations, the question arises: can a professionalism be derived that has authority, however tenuous, however fragile?

My argument here will take the form of *three theses*: first, that the *challenge* to professionalism lies in the handling of multiple discourses; second, that the *task* of professionalism lies in the critical deployment of discourses; and third, that the *achievement* of professionalism lies in discursive creation.

The end of conventional categories

In identifying the substance of any such problems before us, we may start indeed with the observation that we live in a 'liquid' world but then go on to observe that the world is fluid to such a degree that conventional categories are rendered at least suspect. The professional person is supposed to know things but problems immediately present themselves. It is not just the familiar observation that particular 'known' facts about the world are often quickly overtaken; there is also the so-called 'redundancy' problem, in which old knowledge needs to be discarded rather like a worn-out motor-car. Just like the motor-car, knowledge has a life, so we are told, and its lifespan is reducing. It is also that the professional role itself is losing its clarity. In the digital age, the client – at least to some extent – can teach the professional, for the client may well have conducted their enquiries on the Internet. The pedagogical balance of the professional–client relationship changes.

At the same time, in a marketised age, in which clients are able to 'shop around' for services, the client is less dependent on any individual professional. So the economic balance of the relationship also changes. In turn, this economic re-ordering is likely to have an impact on the epistemological authority of the professional. If the client can simply up-sticks and go elsewhere, the sage-like character of the professional's pronouncements dissipates, for those pronouncements are now received in a 'what-if' mode by the client: '"What if" what I am hearing turns out to be inadequate or even false, when I have checked it out down the road?' may be the thinking of the client.

Accordingly, the old narratives of professional life weaken. Part of the underpinnings of professionalism lay in the concepts of knowledge and truth. It was the professional's role to come to know things and to utilise that knowledge so as to seek the truth in the situations which he or she faced, working disinterestedly in the service of the client. But in a liquid age, representations of the world – which the professionals were good at and which gave the professionals a sense of security – are now hedged in on all sides. The professionals' expertise allowed professionals to speak out. Now, if they do so, they are liable to be called to account; for instance, for writing to the editor on official letterhead paper. After all, their readings of the world are liable to contend against, if only implicitly, the official views of the world.

More than that, more than this phenomenon of the *regulated professional* (as we may term it), professionals now find themselves beset with alternative voices providing rival readings of the world. Not only do contrasting and even hostile narratives issue forth from all manner of 'interest' groups but also their professional 'colleagues' will be liable to be writing in the next issue of the profession's journal, with a different interpretation of events.

Modern life, we may observe, is one of contrasting and alternative discourses. And these discourses slide across each other. Consequently, the very ideas of 'profession', 'professionalism' and 'professional life' fade from view and even dissolve, as they are overtaken by other swifter currents – of entrepreneurialism, of management, of quality assurance and even of 'client satisfaction'. The discourses mingle. Sometimes, the mingling does not go far; like oil and water, they stay separate even if interlaced. At other times, like olive oil and vinegar, they really do mingle, but then they find the co-existence difficult and go back to their separate formations.

Under these circumstances, it is difficult if not impossible for professionals to hold onto their epistemological authority. There are two distinct challenges, as we have just seen. On the one hand, there is the challenge of 'I know as much as you' or 'You don't know as much as you pretend to know'. In the knowledge society, everyone is knowledgeable to some extent or – even more significantly – can very quickly get themselves up to speed on any topic that they fancy. So the advice of the professional is sought not so much because they have an arcane knowledge but simply because it saves time: with a little effort, the client can begin to feel that they could step into the shoes of the professional. In the knowledge society, what was sacred knowledge is rendered profane and even mundane.

On the other hand, there is the challenge of 'Your knowledge is a self-interested knowledge'. Here, amid the eruption of perspectives in the modern world, professional knowledge comes to be seen as unduly self-protective. It comes to be seen as cloaking itself with a spurious claim to prestige and a self-satisfaction lacking in due modesty. Now, professional knowledge has to fight its corner against a myriad of growing orderings of the world and competing value systems. 'Client satisfaction', 'performance indicators', 'quality of life', 'economic value': these are just some indicators of rival discourses that seek to cabin and confine professional knowledge.

It surely follows, therefore, that the traditional vocabulary of professional life with its dominant categories – of 'knowledge' (and *sotto voce*, 'high status knowledge'), of 'service' and of 'disinterestedness' – can no longer supply the basis of an impregnable discourse. Professional life and its self-understandings are under assault. In the process, the categories of professional life are liable to crumble.

Being a professional in an age of supercomplexity

'Being' was perhaps Heidegger's fundamental category (Heidegger, 1998). 'Being' was a matter of how individuals are in the world, but it was, for Heidegger, also a matter of how an individual stood in time, backwards and forwards. Being has 'possibilities' and is always restlessly searching, working forwards, even if it knows not where or to what. In turn, though, we may say – although I am not sure if Heidegger said this – that this being takes on its form partly through its understandings of the world. Even if we warrant with Heidegger that ontology is more significant than epistemology, still we can admit that they are interrelated.

Here, for our story, we may say that the professional's *understandings* of him- or herself in the world may profoundly affect his or her *being in the world*. This interconnection between knowing the world and being-in-the-world may be seen as a particular feature of the phenomenon of 'supercomplexity' (Barnett, 2000). 'Supercomplexity' is a condition of multiplying and contending frameworks of understanding. It dislodges categories by which the world is framed, but by no means presents us with new definite categories. Rather, life is now reflexively thrown into a situation of fragility; that is to say, the fragility is itself recognised as being a feature of life itself.

Under conditions *merely of complexity*, professionals experience – for example – systems overload. It is not merely that, for the doctor, say, there are new drugs coming onto the market that have to be comprehended but it is also that their interactions have to be understood. At the same time, the doctor is bombarded with an expanding list of patients (who will be diverse in their ethnic origins and in their religious affiliations), with neverending new regulations, codes and standards to observe, with unpredictable numbers and kinds of data and information (not to mention unsolicited emails) and with new performance measures and responsibilities (such as the budgeting of professional practice). This is a condition of complexity in that the entities impact upon each other and exceed the capacity of the systems to handle them (cf. Beck, 1992). Such conditions of complexity are real, and impose stress both on the systems and on doctors themselves (who might even be considered to form part of the systems). A feature of such conditions of complexity is that, to some degree, they could be resolved given more resources (time, money, data, staff). Conditions of complexity, stressful as they may be, are to a significant extent *in principle* capable of resolution.

Conditions of supercomplexity, on the other hand, are not capable of resolution in any such way. They do not permit, even in principle, any kind of technical or systems fix. For conditions of complexity are in essence marked by the question 'Who am I?' or, here and less prosaically: 'What is to count as professionalism?' Such questions are characteristically open-ended or even 'essentially contested'. Their logic is that, in themselves, they invite contending responses. But more than that, they are also *contingently* contested. That is to say, in the contemporary world, with its multiple perspectives and interests – emphasised by globalisation – multiple and contending responses to such open-ended questions crowd in as a matter of fact. As a matter of fact, and not only of logic, the hard-pressed professional is faced with an identity crisis. Is professionalism a matter of being a knowledgeable expert or of meeting clients' wants or of managing resources efficiently or of entrepreneurial nous? Is it a private, a public, a bureaucratic or a performative mode of being that is called for?

To put things this way is to say that the actual social character of professionalism trumps the philosophy of professionalism. Both are important – in the one, we see into the actual dilemmas facing the professional, while in the other, we open a space for new imaginings – but the former is the more important for our story here. For the former, the sociology of professionalism, bears in – we might even say – on the soul of professionalism. Whereas the logical and conceptual dimensions of professionalism may send illuminating shafts of insight and present with even disturbing considerations, the sociology of professionalism lays bare the *actualité* of professional life, warts and all (to coin a phrase).

It is not that the sociological account is more critical than the philosophical account. Indeed, the philosophical account may be devastatingly critical in coming forward with new concepts of professional life that furnish disturbing vistas, as gaps between the real and the imaginary are revealed. Nor is it that the sociological account is in itself necessarily more personal than the philosophical account. For the philosophical enterprise, in furnishing new and even critical concepts, can itself have profound ontological impacts. There may be nothing more powerful or even revolutionary than a clear and penetrating concept. It is rather that the social aspects of supercomplexity bear in upon the professional in a particularly pressing way. The professional is – as a matter of fact – called to account daily, almost minute by minute. And by 'called to account' here we have to mean giving an account of oneself to different callings, different evocations, of the professional role – as the professional turns in the space of an hour from a client and quasi-market relationship to a peer and expert relationship (in the phone call to a colleague over a particularly technical matter) and then to a bureaucratic mode (as the proforma from the national authority is completed).

The being, therefore, of the professional is severely tested nowadays. This is understood to be a continuing part of the professional life. A characteristically modern way of putting the point might be to suggest that the professional now lives with multiple identities. I think that that must be right but that way of putting it surely does not do justice to the situation. Here, perhaps, terminology either taken from or provoked by Heidegger may be helpful. In the contemporary world, the professional's 'comportment' and 'possibilities' are unsettled. 'Authenticity' becomes problematic. There is here a set of dislocations between the professional and the world. Or rather, the professional's hold on the world or, as we may put it, her 'here-and-nowness' lacks anchor. But nor is it free-floating. For there are real forces at work, in which the professional is oriented this way and that – if only in the language that she or he utters.

This is precisely the set of challenges of being a professional in an age of supercomplexity. Under such conditions, the professional neither has his or her 'professionalism' given in any real sense but nor has carte blanche to shape it. Higher expectations among clients, evermore explicit standards articulated by professional bodies, and an evolving policy framework developed by the state, not to mention the growing interestedness and even involvement of the wider community: all conspire to orient professional life in certain directions, which may even be mutually incompatible. At the same time, there may be a fuzziness to this boundary setting and direction pointing. So the being of the professional is caught amid tensions and fluidity.

The is/ought problem

It could be said that professionalism is hollowing out. Especially in the 'public sector', professionals are being expected to meet performance targets and to take on responsibilities in relation to income generation and so acquire a management function. These shifts are real shifts for they affect the professional–client relationship: now, the client is construed under performance categories (of throughput, cost and output).

Amid these processes, the language of professionalism changes. From a language of 'trust', 'integrity', 'commitment' and 'loyalty', currents run that would funnel in a new language of 'efficiency', 'performance indicators', 'standards', being 'adaptable' and managing in a 'smart' fashion. Putting the matter crisply, we might say that professionalism is witnessing a lurch from an ethic of service to an ethic of performance.

If such a change is happening, a problem arises over the ethics of professionalism. The problem can be put in the following, even if somewhat opaque, way: is the 'ought' in the horizon of the 'is' *or* is the 'is' in the horizon of the 'ought'? Let us briefly tease out this cryptic question.

If professionalism now lies in an ethic of performance rather than an ethic of service then professionalism becomes a matter of getting by, of getting on, of visibility, of demonstrable achievement. This professionalism is evident in its coping with the press of the moment, in all its complexity. This professionalism deals with what is the case, the here-and-now. It is true that it might extend itself to thinking strategically, in drawing up plans for the next few years and in trying to anticipate the future. But this strategic thinking – and its ally, strategic action – is still intent on performance as such. This ethic of performance is a hollowed-out ethic. It is not really an ethic at all. It feels uncomfortable at talk of values; squeamish even. Values cannot appear, it may seem, in its bottom line. It would rather press on, having little or no truck with values as such.

In the old days, professionals could content themselves that they were value-driven. They started from a value position – around service, disinterestedness, a concern with truthfulness and integrity – and built their professional practices on that value base. Their actions, and their intentions, only gained sense in that value-laden context. The 'is' of professional life had its place in the horizon of the 'ought'. What ought to be done set a tight frame around what was done. Professional life was securely and assuredly an ethical set of practices.

Now, though, in the new professionalism, the dimension of the 'ought' (What ought I to do? What ought professionals in general to do?) fades. It can only gain an appearance against the horizon of what is the case. Let us get on with the problems facing us today and then turn to value issues – if there is any time left at the end of the day.

So, our earlier question insists upon itself. Does the 'is' of professional life still find its place against the horizon of the 'ought' *or* is it now the case that the 'ought' has given way to the 'is' of professional life and only finds its place, if at all, against the horizon of the 'is'? The 'is' – the *realpolitik* – of professional life has, it may seem, become dominant; the 'ought' scratches around even to have a presence, let alone a hearing. 'Ought' questions are barely tolerated now, it may appear. They are surplus to requirements. They just get in the way of effective practice.

Of course, things are not this simple. However much it may seem as if the old has been vanquished, as a matter of fact, it lives on, by and large. It is still there; not especially visible perhaps. It does not want to frighten the horses, or get itself undue attention. So it recedes into the background, practising its craft quietly and discreetly. This old guard may even find ways of meeting up from time to time, in occasional conferences or seminars.

In such a situation, values jostle: the new and the traditional. But are these different sets of values compatible or incompatible? Are the values of professionalism widening – the new and the traditional being held together – or are the different sets of values such that they never could be combined? The value situation of professionalism could be felt to be like an optical illusion: it is either a duck or a rabbit but not both in the same image.

The modern professional can be forgiven if she or he feels like a small animal caught in the headlights of an oncoming car at night-time. There it was, minding its own business, going about its tasks in its own way, and now it has an apparent juggernaut – of performativity – bearing down on it. How is it to react? How can it react? What *ought* it to do? Survival only seems possible if it succumbs and allows itself to be swept up and carried forth. Indeed, stopping to think about what it *ought* to do will spell disaster; it had better just give itself up to what *is* assuredly the case.

So the is–ought problem of professionalism is real; it is not merely a philosophical conundrum. It compounds the uncertainty that the professional is already feeling. The handling of *this* uncertainty is yet another feature of being a professional in an age of supercomplexity.

Two theses – a challenge and a task

I said at the outset that I wanted to press three theses. We are now, I think, in a position to argue the first two of those theses, which are namely that:

- the *challenge* to professionalism lies in the handling of multiple discourses

- the *task* of professionalism lies in the critical deployment of discourses.

Common to both of these theses is the idea of discourse. I take 'discourse' to refer to a set of structured and collective representations of the world. On that definition, it is surely clear – at least, from our discussion here – that a fundamental challenge to professionalism lies in the handling of multiple discourses. Professionals are caught amid multiple discourses that pivot variously around themes such as service, performance, marketability, client satisfaction, and knowledge and truth. These discourses, as we have noted, are in tension between themselves. Being a professional is not easy these days, therefore. The conscientious professional ducks and dives amid multiple discourses. The 'who am I' question presses itself forward. Self-understanding becomes a continuing and fraught project, for the different discourses reflexively present back oneself in different lights. So we can reiterate, and with some confidence, that indeed *the challenge to professionalism lies in the handling of multiple discourses*.

But professionals are complex beings. They are used to making things up as they go along, to quite a large extent, even if within the frame of ethical codes. The concept of 'responsibility' has application to professional life in part because professionals have pools of autonomy in which they are obliged to make choices, albeit in the interests at least of their clients. Professionals live for 'the other', that is to say that they live their working lives partly in the interests of realms outside themselves – their clients' well-being, their profession itself, and their fulfilment of professional commitments. Their motivation may be flagging at any period in their lives or they may just be a little unwell but still they keep going. Being professional is playing out one's professional services even as one's own psyche, quite apart from the immediate environment, points in other directions.

All this is to say that professionals are both inner-directed and outer-directed all at once. They are surrounded by and immersed in different accounts of their responsibilities; different discourses indeed. However, the ethical space in which they move, one of personal responsibility, not merely allows but enjoins them to take up deliberative stances towards those discourses. At times, they will feel under siege as they find certain discourses working against the grain of their own values; or, to put it differently, their own favoured discourses.

Being professional in this situation, as we have just observed, requires a handling of multiple and even rival discourses. But the fully fledged professional will be engaging with those discourses. Having his or her own value position, and favouring some discourses rather than others, the professional will be evaluating discourses, even if intuitively. This is a critical professional who ducks and dives amid discourses but does so not totally aimlessly but strategically. This professional tries to steer a discursive path that has some boundaries to it. There may be no end-point but this professional does not allow herself to be entirely subject to the manifold discourses that beset her. She engages critically with the discourses she encounters. She goes further: she deploys discourses to help her achieve her own ends. Certainly, some discourses in the contemporary age insist upon themselves and they are backed by some big battalions.

Their force is real. But our fully engaged professional keeps pressing on, using her own favoured discourses with discretion as she manoeuvres a path through the discursive thickets. Accordingly, our *second thesis* may be reiterated with some level of justification, namely that *the task of professionalism lies in the critical deployment of discourses*.

Practising professionalism

Scary images of contemporary professionalism are to be found in the literature, so scary that we may be forgiven for believing that the very idea of professionalism is now otiose. After all, the suggestion that professionals have been 'proletarianised' (Halsey, 1992) precisely gains its purchase from a sense that professionals are no longer able to determine the conditions of their own labour. Professionals are so encircled by rules, regulations and requirements that are not of their own making, that they now take on the appearance of a proletariat, whose conditions of labour are determined outside themselves.

Extraordinarily, Halsey was speaking of the academic 'profession', perceiving a 'decline' in 'donnish dominion', and partly from the perspective of an Oxford don at that. Halsey's use of the term 'don' itself refers to an elite within an elite that surely retains considerable freedoms and autonomy. 'Proletarianisation', we may accordingly judge, is relative: it depends from what vantage point the observation is being made and who is doing the observing. So the more dismal accounts of the decline of professionalism may just tell us more about the commentator than about the nature of professions and professionalism themselves.

Still, our account so far has been in part one of growing challenges upon professionals and the exercise of their professionalism. Expectations and forms of accountability multiply and even conflict. And the stories written about professionals also multiply, both

actually (on the front pages of newspapers) and more discursively (the narratives also grow and sheer away from each other). The ground of the professional's being, qua professional, gives way; the professional is undermined.

So our account is different from Halsey's. Whereas, for Halsey, professionals have seen diminished their autonomy to determine the conditions of their own labour, on the survey of this chapter we can say that the undermining of professionalism is a larger story about the complexity of modern life. Professionalism, as we earlier observed, is being 'hollowed out', since what it is to be a professional is no longer clear. Here, the loss of autonomy that is the result of a regulatory state taking a closer interest in professional life (and in some professions in particular) is simply part of that larger depiction of the multiplying and often mutually contesting sets of expectations that befall the professional.

In such a milieu, professionalism takes on a nice aspect. Old-style professionalism cannot be practised in any straightforward way; professional angst has its point. But the values that are associated with old-style professionalism – of independence, critical reason, communication, a disinterested attention to a set of standards outside oneself – still linger. The idea of the professional attending to a calling remains in the professional ether. The being of the professional is now layered, as the different voices – with their differing degrees of urgency – are heard. Performativity, service, criticality, truthfulness – all these and more jostle as counter-claims upon the professional. Accordingly, an authentic professionalism now resides in the traditional values of professionalism coming to the rescue. The multiplicity of callings, and of voices and, indeed, of discourses that bear in upon professionalism cannot be gainsaid. But the true professional will now play with these discourses, as a playwright brings on different characters at different times.

We can now reassert and claim again our third thesis: namely, that the achievement of professionalism lies in discursive creation. The professional in the contemporary era has to be creative; has to become the *creative* professional. Creativity is apparent at three levels. First, the critical deployment of discourses – our second thesis – itself requires a minimal level of creativity. Professional criticality is an indication of an attempt to retain a measure of autonomy amid the swirling currents that beset professionals; or, at least, those who would see themselves as professionals. This is not exactly a passive creativity, for creativity never could be passive. But it is rather a merely responsive creativity in that it is a creativity that works at the maintenance of the individual ego. At a second and higher level, creativity is itself spontaneous. It is even – to draw on a neologism – *proactive*. This creativity refuses to be bound in and succumb to a regulated professionalism but strikes out to achieve its own projects. It is even 'entrepreneurial'.

A third level of creativity is still yet available to professionals. In this third level of creativity, the professional recalls her ethical callings. She recognise the inevitable 'oughtnesses' of her situation. Her service to her clients; her truthfulness, both technically and morally (in being honest and straightforward in difficult settings); her discipline and her profession: all these call the professional forward into acting within boundaries – at once of respect, of knowledge and truth, and of faithfulness to epistemic and professional communities. At the same time, every situation that the professional encounters has particular characteristics and so the professional has to think morally on her feet. There are no moral blueprints on which the professional can fall back. The professional has to deploy a level of practical wisdom. This is the basis of the ethical profession. But this is a demanding role that itself calls for creativity in which the professional works through options and even dilemmas, the identification of which themselves call for creativity.

This is an authentic professionalism, even if the authenticity in question is never quite achieved. It is always the nearly possible; always just out of reach. Whereas our first (ego maintenance) and second (project realisation) levels of creativity can be realised, at least in principle, this third level of creativity never could be completely realised. The ethical professional is always struggling to do well in her moral engagements. 'Doing well' here has two sides to it. On the one hand, the ethical professional struggles to keep faith with her clients and others, all the while making judgements as to the extent to which keeping faith is justified. Even a client may forfeit such faith. On the other hand, the value dilemmas that our professional identifies never could be completely resolved: they have to be held in some kind of tension.

But what – as in our third thesis – of '*discursive* creation'? I would want to suggest that professional creativity of the kind we have intimated is *ipso facto* a matter of discursive creation. We have seen that, in effect, the professional is caught amid swirling discourses, the currents of which may flow in different directions. From one moment to another, the professional finds herself caught in particular discourses. In some settings – the professional workshop, the team meeting – multiple discourses may break in, in juxtaposed or even in single utterances. The modern professional cannot help but be part of a mélange of discourses.

We have said, too, that the realisation of professionalism involves not merely the handling of these multiple discourses but also in their critical deployment. Here, though, we are making the further move: namely, that the realisation of professionalism lies in discursive creation. For this thoroughly modern professional will not rest even with critically deploying discourses and placing her own stamp on them but will become so energised that she will be discursively creative. She will find ways of so engaging with contending audiences in energising her projects that new social relationships, new networks, new groupings may well be formed. In the process, in the slipping and sliding between interest groups, some well established, some in the process of formation, our professional will be part of a quasi-political process in which new ideas and new projects are levered forward.

Inevitably, all this will require discursive creation. New groupings and new cross-cutting interrelationships are formed. This is less of a hybrid grouping than a grouping of many leanings. And our professional becomes naturally adept at finding, at working out, a language in which many, if not all, of the contending parties can participate. Our modern professional is so realising her professionalism that she naturally becomes a creator of new discourses; or at least, helps to nurture those discourses and – albeit with others – helps to give them sustaining strength. Hence our third thesis can be reasserted with surely some level of confidence: that the achievement of professionalism lies in discursive creation.

Conclusion

The modern professional – if we are to do any justice to the phrase – has to be both a practising epistemologist *and* a practising ontologist. On the one hand, she has to know things and go on knowing; and to practise what she preaches; and find new things to preach. That is obvious enough: the professional is a living project of knowledge in action. On the other hand, the professional, it has surely become clear in our explorations in this chapter, also has to take on – on a daily basis – the task of making herself in the world. And this making of the professional self is bound up with moments of criticality and discursive formation. The professional lives amid, and contributes to, in critical fashion, the development of professional discourses. In the process, she makes herself anew and continuingly so. Accordingly, this modern professional professes as much in her mode of being – is seen to be critically creative amid the craziness of her world – as it is in her moments of overt knowledge creation.

Certainly, this kind of professionalism is fragile; its watchwords are eternal vigilance and courageous action. Knowing, acting and communicating, and in a spirit of criticality: all this and on a daily basis. No wonder that professionals often seek early retirement. But that many continue for decades is testimony to the possibility of professionalism in the modern age. The idea of a critical professionalism in an age of supercomplexity can be more than an idea.

References

Barnett, R. (2000) *Realizing the University in an Age of Supercomplexity*. Buckingham: Open University Press.

Bauman, Z. (2000) *Liquid Modernity*. Cambridge: Polity.

Beck, U. (1992) *Risk Society: Towards a New Modernity*. London: Sage.

Halsey, A.H. (1992) *Decline of Donnish Dominion*. Oxford: Clarendon.

Heidegger, M. (1998) *Being and Time*. Oxford: Blackwell.

Index